T0323819

"Refreshing and relatable. A must-read for those who want a foundation of this evidence-based model's rich history combined with a hands-on understanding of its powerful application in the present. Yvonne Dolan brings this model to life with stories, examples, and research, making this a book you can't afford to miss."

Teri Pichot, LCSW, LAC, MAC, *Clinical Director of Denver Center for Solution-Focused Brief Therapy, U.S.A., author of* Solution-Focused Substance Abuse Treatment, *and* Solution-Focused Brief Therapy: Its Effective Use in Agency Settings

"Yvonne Dolan captures the heart and soul of solution-focused practice, engaging the reader in an inspiring and compelling journey from the beginning of its development to its practical applications in many diverse areas. A training faculty member of the original Brief Family Therapy Center (BFTC), the home of solution-focused brief therapy, Yvonne is the most authoritative voice today. This is an absolute 'must have' book for those who are curious about, teach or practice the solution-focused approach."

Debbie Hogan, MS, MSFC, ICF-MCC, EMCC MP, EMCC ESIA, *Director of the Academy of Solution Focused Training, Singapore, author of* Solution Focused Practice in Asia

"Yvonne Dolan's new book is 'a must' for any SF practitioner's bookshelf. It stands apart from most other SF texts in that it takes a real 'nuts and bolts', 'drilling-down' approach to how SF conversations work in a variety of settings. Also, there is one of the clearest descriptions I have seen yet, of what makes SF radically different from other ways of working."

John Hendon, *Director of John Hendon Consultancy, UK, author of* Preventing Suicide: The Solution Focused Approach, *and* Beating Combat Stress: 101 Techniques for Recovery

"This highly readable book is crystal clear evidence of a theoretical-practical SFT alliance in which core elements and key assumptions form the pragmatic, linguistic and philosophical heart and soul of the SFT approach with an eye to its genesis and development. Each chapter is larded with clear examples using a variety of SFT techniques and explanations applicable in a variety of settings."

Jos Kienhuis, *Head of European Brief Therapy Association Research Task Group, Director of Jos Kienhuis Consultancy, the Netherlands*

SOLUTION-FOCUSED THERAPY

This book presents the fundamentals of the evidence-based solution-focused brief therapy approach by examining how it was developed, the research that supports it, and the key techniques that enable its effective implementation.

Developed originally as a psychotherapeutic approach, the solution-focused approach is now being applied across a wide variety of contexts including psychotherapy and counseling, schools, business, and organisations. This accessible and introductory guide provides a unified description and demonstration of the basic commonalities that characterise, inform, and support its implementation across all these contexts. Readers will acquire a clear understanding of the essentials of the solution-focused approach and how to apply it to everyday life.

This book is essential for undergraduate students in courses such as psychotherapy, clinical psychology, and social work. As well as mental health professionals and caregivers seeking to quickly familiarise themselves with the solution-focused approach, and anyone interested in solution-focused and brief therapies.

Yvonne Dolan is a Solution-Focused Therapy practitioner, consultant, and trainer in the United States. She has provided training on the solution-focused approach in 22 countries. She is also the author/co-author of 7 books, numerous chapters, and articles, and her writing has been translated into 8 languages.

The Basics Series

The Basics is a highly successful series of accessible guidebooks which provide an overview of the fundamental principles of a subject area in a jargon-free and undaunting format.

Intended for students approaching a subject for the first time, the books both introduce the essentials of a subject and provide an ideal springboard for further study. With over 50 titles spanning subjects from artificial intelligence (AI) to women's studies, *The Basics* are an ideal starting point for students seeking to understand a subject area.

Each text comes with recommendations for further study and gradually introduces the complexities and nuances within a subject.

TRANSLATION
Juliane House

WORK PSYCHOLOGY
Laura Dean and Fran Cousans

ECONOMICS (fourth edition)
Tony Cleaver

ELT
Michael McCarthy and Steve Walsh

SOLUTION-FOCUSED THERAPY
Yvonne Dolan

ACTING (third edition)
Bella Merlin

For a full list of titles in this series, please visit www.routledge.com/The-Basics/book-series/B

SOLUTION-FOCUSED THERAPY

THE BASICS

Yvonne Dolan

Routledge
Taylor & Francis Group

NEW YORK AND LONDON

Designed cover image: andipantz ©Getty Images

First published 2024
by Routledge
605 Third Avenue, New York, NY 10158

and by Routledge
4 Park Square, Milton Park, Abingdon, Oxon, OX14 4RN

Routledge is an imprint of the Taylor & Francis Group, an informa business

ISBN: 978-1-032-51131-3 (hbk)
ISBN: 978-1-032-51129-0 (pbk)
ISBN: 978-1-003-40123-0 (ebk)

DOI: 10.4324/9781003401230

Typeset in Bembo
by MPS Limited, Dehradun

This book is dedicated to my husband,
Terry Trepper.

CONTENTS

ACKNOWLEDGMENTS
(SFT: THE BASICS)

Let it suffice to say that if I mentioned every colleague whose knowledge has benefitted me over the years, the resulting acknowledgments would necessarily be longer than this book!

First of all, I want to especially thank my wonderful husband, Terry Trepper, whose scholarly research, editorial skills, warm personal support and early morning coffee were invaluable.

I also want to thank my editor, Sarah Rae and her editorial assistant, Pragati Sharma at Taylor and Francis.

I am permanently indebted to my longtime mentors and dear friends, the late Insoo Kim Berg and the late Steve de Shazer whose writing, teaching, and ongoing professional guidance permanently changed my work and life perspective. Further, my understanding of the SFT approach benefitted greatly from the research and scholarly writings of the original team at the Milwaukee Brief Family Center (Steve de Shazer, Insoo Kim Berg, Eve Lipchik, Wally Gingerich, Michele Weiner-Davis, Jim Derks, Gale Miller, and the late Elam Nunnally).

Additionally, I have been repeatedly and variously inspired by the writing, work, unique perspectives, and training programs of numerous highly skilled SF colleagues over the years. Foremost among these are Harry and Jocelyn Korman, Myriam Le Fevere de Ten Hove, Debbie and Dave Hogan, Cynthia Franklin, Ben Furman, Eric McCollum, Peter Sundman, Kirsten Dierolf, Peter Szabo, Karen Sands, Insa Sparrer, Mathias Varga von Kibed, Harvey Ratner, Chris Iveson, Evan George, Heather Fiske, Teri Pichot, Johnny Kim, Sara Smock

Jordan, Cynthia Franklin, John Henden, Michael Durrant, Manfred Vogt, Haesun Moon, Heinrich Dreesen, Sarah Smock Therese Steiner, Mo Yee Lee, Mark Beyebach, Frederik LinBen, Peter de Jong, Penney Griffiths, Marie-Christine Cabie, Ben Furman, Jos Kienhuis, John Wheeler, Ferdinand Wolf, the late Luc Isebaert, the late Karel Buitinga, the late Charlie Johnson, and the late Janet Bavelas.

WHAT IS SOLUTION-FOCUSED THERAPY AND HOW WAS IT DEVELOPED?

Solution-Focused Therapy (SFT)[1], was first developed in the early 1980s as a brief psychotherapy model. Since then, solution-focused (SF) techniques and principles have expanded to become a major influence in a variety of settings all over the world ranging from education, social policy, and business in addition to social work, counseling psychology, and psychiatry (Trepper et al., 2006). Although originally created in an outpatient mental health clinic, it is not necessary to be a mental health professional to learn about the approach and use the helpful and innovative ideas that characterise it. For our purposes throughout this book we will refer to *solution-focused practices* when referring to more general applications of the approach and the more specific *solution-focused therapy* when referring specifically to application of the counseling and psychotherapy.

The purpose of this chapter is to offer a clear definition of the SFT approach, from which the more general solution-focused practices emerged, to describe how, where, when, and by whom it was developed, to introduce the core techniques used to implement it, and to summarise the research that demonstrates its validity as an evidence-based approach. This is followed by a chapter content summary, a glossary of key terms, and a conclusion with an optional exercise

---

[1]Often referred to as Solution-Focused Brief Therapy (SFBT)

DOI: 10.4324/9781003401230-1

designed to provide firsthand experience of the way of thinking that characterises the heart of the SF approach.

WHAT EXACTLY IS SOLUTION-FOCUSED THERAPY?

Solution-Focused Therapy (SFT) is a future-focused, goal–directed, evidence-based brief therapy approach that helps people and organisations achieve change by creating *solutions* rather than focusing on *problems* and the events that led to them (de Shazer et al., 2007; 2021; Kim et al., 2010; 2019). Put in plain language, SFT is a highly practical, future–oriented conversational method that motivates and empowers people to develop lasting solutions by focusing directly on desired changes instead of dwelling on the problem. When not being used specifically in psychotherapy settings, the approach and specific techniques are collectively referred to as solution-focused practices. For example, attorneys may use solution–focused practices while engaging in divorce mediation (Bannink, 2008).

Although most people do not initially realise it, elements of their desired solution, known as **exceptions,** are usually already present in some aspect of their life and their behavioral experience. In SFT, exceptions are the basis for ongoing change and the primary resource for creatively developing highly personal, effective, and sustainable solutions.

WHAT MAKES SFT DIFFERENT FROM OTHER APPROACHES?

SFT is a major paradigm shift from traditional psychotherapy, which almost universally focuses on *problem* formation and *problem* resolution. Instead, SFT focuses on client *strengths*, *resiliencies*, and *exceptions* to the problem and then, through various interventions, encourages clients to do more of those behaviors. While SFT is known for its many unique techniques, they are all based on the foundational principal that clients ultimately know what is best for themselves and have the ability to effectively plan how to get there (Trepper et al., 2006). Thus, the client is always seen as the "expert," with the job of the practitioner being to help elicit change by helping the client recognise their own expertise, exceptions to their problems, and previous solutions.

SF practices differ from most other approaches to psychotherapy and behavioral change in a number of other ways, including: 1) The way it was originally developed; 2) The tenets and assumptions that SF practitioners use to inform their work; and 3) The uniquely collaborative techniques SF practitioners use to co-develop practical solutions with their clients (Solution Focused Brief Therapy Association, 2013). Another distinguishing quality of the SF approach is that it generates more positive emotions during the counseling process and after than problem-focused approaches (Kim et al., 2022).

SFT originated *inductively*, that is from direct observation of real-life clients, rather than *deductively* or based on theory as most traditional psychotherapies historically were. SFT is one of the only psychotherapy approaches in the world that was "evidence-based" from its earliest beginnings. SFT was developed by observing clinical sessions firsthand in order to discover what worked best and figure out how to replicate it. As a result, SFT is an essentially an active, pragmatic approach rather than a theoretical model (Lipchik et al., 2012).

The practical common-sense quality of the SFT approach is probably also related to the location of the outpatient clinic where its developers made their observations: The Milwaukee, Wisconsin, inner city neighborhoods populated by working class families and people variously struggling with drug dependence, homelessness, and chronic, untreated mental illness. Given this environment, it is not surprising that one of the most defining aspects of the SFT approach is its strong emphasis on formulating practical, meaningful goals directly based on clients' best hopes for improving their everyday real-life situations.

THE EARLY DEVELOPMENT OF SFT

The SFT approach grew directly from the work of the Steve de Shazer (1940–2005) and Insoo Kim Berg (1934–2007), along with their team of colleagues and students at the Brief Family Therapy Center in Milwaukee, Wisconsin (BFTC). In addition to serving as an outpatient clinic, BFTC also functioned as a training institute for students and colleagues who wanted to learn SFT. The original BFTC group included Jim Derks, Elam Nunnally, Marilyn La Court and Eve Lipchik, and their students included (among many others), John Walter, Jane Peller, Michele Weiner-Davis and Yvonne Dolan (the author of this book).

Every session at BFTC was recorded for research purposes. Along with their team of colleagues and students, Berg and de Shazer observed thousands and thousands of both live and recorded therapy sessions over the course of several years. During this time they kept careful records of any type of any question, statement, or behavior on the part of the therapist that consistently led to clients reporting positive outcome. They also made follow-up calls to their clients to find out if the therapy sessions had actually been helpful.

The process was quite straightforward: The questions, statements, and activities that were repeatedly associated with clients reporting progress were carefully incorporated into the SFT approach. Any statements, questions, or other behaviors on the part the therapist that did *not* prove to be associated with therapeutic improvement were eliminated from their evolving approach. This may now seem like an obvious procedure for the best clinical results. However, this was virtually unheard of in the clinical landscape of that time, which was instead driven by strict adherence to theoretical constructs of psychoanalysis and behavioral therapy, then the two dominant approaches.

In order to fully understand how such a dramatic paradigm shift in psychotherapy came into being, it will be helpful to look at the personal and professional backgrounds of the two primary architects of the SFT approach: Married partners Steve de Shazer and Insoo Kim Berg. They dedicated their lives to developing SFT and training SFT practitioners in the approach all over the world.

Having had the good fortune to enjoy a close friendship and work relationship with Insoo and Steve for over twenty years in which we co-authored books, traveled, and taught workshops together all over the world, shared countless long walks, and sometimes even cooked meals together, I (YD) now take this opportunity to offer a firsthand sketch of the creative interests and personal backgrounds they brought to the development of SFT. As you will see, Steve De Shazer and Insoo Kim Berg were every bit as unique as the SFT approach they developed.

Steve de Shazer

The son of an electrician father and an opera singer mother, Steve de Shazer was both highly creative and eminently pragmatic, an intellectual who also liked sports cars, detective stories, researching international recipes, and cooking gourmet Asian food for his family and friends. He was also an abstract painter with a university degree in fine arts, and an accomplished professional saxophonist. Prior to earning his MSW degree in Social Work, Shazer earned his living performing in a jazz band throughout the US; he had played with a number of famous jazz musicians including Eric Dolphy, Tito Barbieri, and Count Basie, and was a devoted fan of Thelonious Monk. An unusually attentive, sensitive listener, de Shazer confided that he found Monk's music so completely absorbing that he could not risk driving a car while listening to his recordings. De Shazer was also devoted baseball fan who regularly attended Brewers game whenever he was home in Milwaukee.

In addition to all these other interests, de Shazer was also a serious scholar. He had made in-depth studies of philosopher Ludwig Wittgenstein's writings on linguistics and logic, was intrigued by all the most recent developments Brief Family Therapy movement in his own field, and was constantly exploring ideas from sociology, anthropology, and communication theorists about various ways to influence positive change.

Perhaps due to his social work background and appreciation of the importance of social justice, Steve de Shazer tended to be highly critical of *theory-driven* treatment approaches that did not reliably result in people getting better, particularly ones that took a long time, cost a great deal of money and lacked substantial clinical research proving their efficacy. Firm in his belief that all human beings were by definition unique individuals, he categorically objected to "one size fits all" psychotherapy approaches that failed to acknowledge and utilise the unique experiences, hopes, and strengths that characterised each person.

Insoo Kim Berg

Born and raised in South Korea, Insoo Kim Berg and her family witnessed horrific suffering, enduring severe hardship and traumatic loss during the Korean War. Insoo's father played an important role in her intellectual development. In contrast to her mother, who Insoo described as "a very traditionally minded woman who believed women should be primarily taught how to be competent wives and mothers," Insoo's father, the owner of a large pharmaceutical business, believed that his daughters should receive the same level of university education as his sons. He arranged for both Insoo and her sister to receive university educations that were highly unusual for South Korean women of their generation.

Insoo's education made her curious about the larger world and led her to seek permission to study in the US. Although Insoo's mother was reluctant about letting her go, her father prevailed and gave her permission to travel to the US to attend the University of Wisconsin in Milwaukee.

Although she described herself as "not religious by nature," Insoo told me that her way of thinking and overall view of life were influenced by the Buddhist philosophy and principles she had naturally absorbed while growing in the South Korean culture. Her way of approaching adversity became especially evident during a teaching trip to South Korea in which Insoo and I trained all of the homeless women's shelter workers in the country. That particular trip had involved a particularly grueling schedule sandwiched between long international flights. It was the Asian winter cold and flu season, and Insoo became ill. Complaining was not in Insoo's nature. Well into her 60s, frail and obviously suffering from a bad cold, I knew that she must be really quite ill when she asked me to take over her portion of the teaching for the day.

Although Insoo had completely lost her voice by mid-morning, when I tried to convince her to go back to the hotel to rest, she categorically refused. "I am a strong woman, she responded firmly, "I am definitely staying until the end of the day." Back in our hotel that night, over cups of hot tea and bowls of steamed dumplings, I asked Insoo how she managed to keep working so tirelessly day after day as I had watched her do for years.

> 'Growing up in a Buddhist culture,' she answered, 'you learn to view adversity differently than Westerners; you put one foot in front of the other and then you simply do what you can; you don't get caught up in any unnecessary struggles, you just keep going. And living through the war provided me with a kind of clarity about what really matters, what is ultimately important. For me, it is always people, never things or possessions.' Reflecting on her childhood, Insoo said 'The war was terrible. It left me with a strong desire to try to do what I could help people, to do anything I could to ease the suffering the world.'

Although Insoo personally exemplified the implicitly compassionate stance that characterises the most effective use of the approach, this was only one of several important things she contributed to the development of SFT. Having worked in a pharmaceutical research lab while completing her MSW Social Work degree at the University of Wisconsin, Insoo had a solid understanding of scientific research protocol in addition to a thorough understanding of the theories and techniques that characterised all the mainstream and emerging psychotherapy approaches.

After completing her social worker degree, Insoo studied brief therapy at the Mental Research Institute (MRI) in Palo Alto, California. While studying at MRI, she became acquainted with her future husband, Steve de Shazer. Although he never formally studied at MRI, Steve was a frequent visitor, dropping in regularly to discuss ideas with longtime friends and colleagues John Weakland, Richard Fisch, and Paul Watzlawick. Although both Steve and Insoo were influenced by the ideas about brief therapy they had been introduced to at MRI, it was Insoo's clinical work which inspired the original writings of Steve de Shazer.

Looking back over his career just a few months before he died, Steve confided that a large proportion of what he had written about the SFT approach was a direct reflection of his best efforts to accurately describe how Insoo embodied the approach in her worked with clients. (S. de Shazer, personal communication, August 5, 2005). Having personally spent a lot of time watching Insoo work, I can readily understand while Steve de Shazer made such a concerted effort to make her way of working accessible to others.

The warm, empathic, present-focused manner in which Insoo connected with people seemed completely intuitive, a natural extension of her everyday personality. But the unwavering tenacity she displayed while asking clarifying questions until clients identified a goal that really mattered to them – ones that reflected their best hope – and then collaborated on figuring out exactly how to make it happen was clearly both intentional and deliberate.

Like de Shazer, Insoo Kim Berg was a highly disciplined behavioral scientist and researcher. with a clear mission: Developing practical, effective ways to help people achieve sustainable, practical solutions to real-life problems. And Insoo's personal work ethic was doubtlessly also a significant factor in SFT's successful development. The unflagging energy and dedication with which she approached every project associated with SFT's development was inseparable from who Insoo was as a person.

In addition to authoring countless articles and numerous books translated into several languages, and recording many demonstrations of their clinical work, de Shazer and Berg trained mental health, social service and healthcare professionals all over the world in the SFT approach, and authored numerous books and articles elucidating and demonstrating its application to a wide variety of clinical, social service, educational, and business settings.

AN INTRODUCTION TO THE CORE SF TECHNIQUES

This section will introduce the set of unique techniques SFT practitioners use to implement the approach, with an illustration for each. Although a number of interesting additional techniques have been proposed since the inception of the approach, the descriptions here will be based on those included in the official Solution-Focused Treatment Manual used to standardise clinical research on SFT (Solution-Focused Brief Therapy Association, 2013; Trepper et al., 2012).

Joining with Competencies

In the psychotherapy field, *joining* is the process of creating a therapeutic alliance between the therapist and the client (Panichelli, 2013). Joining includes the ability to initiate and sustain the kind of conversation that makes clients comfortable enough to talk openly about their best goals and best hopes. The skills used to effectively join with clients also have the potential to positively impact one's ability to connect meaningfully with people in one's everyday life, such as family members, friends, students, teachers, co-workers, supervisors, and bosses.

Joining skills are essential to effective SF practices, yet practitioners often struggle with them when first learning the approach, assuming that there is nothing to it, and that they already know how to do it. These newer SF practitioners can mistakenly assume that SFT is just some sort of simplistic, unremittingly positive model instead of the rigorously researched, effective technique-driven, highly pragmatic approach that it is.

Sadly, the previous misconception is not just limited to people outside the mental health field. For example, I once overheard a marriage and family therapist unfamiliar with SFT sarcastically ask a colleague, "Isn't SFT that approach where you just blow sunshine up your clients arses?" While initiating and sustaining a conversation about another person's unique skills, abilities, and resources can initially appear ridiculously simple, requiring little more than knowing how to be "nice" to other people and saying positive things, it actually requires a different skill set than most other kinds of social conversations and even other psychotherapy approaches. Although most people take it for granted that they already know everything necessary to generate and sustain an in-depth conversation primarily focusing on the other person's skills and resources, relatively few people are actually competent and experienced at doing it.

Components of SF Joining

It is important to know when and how to ask the other person about their skills and resources without appearing rudely abrupt or insensitive. The "when" is perhaps the easiest part: SFT practitioners ask about their clients' skills and competencies *as early in a conversation as they can respectfully do so*. But the way you do this can make all the difference in the world. Here are the basic components:

1. **Use a tone and manner that clearly communicates serious interest in hearing what the other person says in answer to questions**. Depending on their current situation, some people require gentle encouragement in order to answer SF questions. Encouragement can be as simple as offering a gentle smile, permission to "take your time" delivered in a reassuring tone of voice, even the simple act of waiting silently to hear their answer. In today's fast paced world, the experience of being patiently listened to is oftentimes an unfamiliar one. People sometimes initially respond with surprise when they realise that the SF practitioner is waiting patiently to hear their answer, e.g., "Sorry – I didn't realise that you actually wanted to hear my answer." Indeed, the experience of being attentively listened to in an appreciative and careful way is becoming an increasingly rare phenomenon.

2. **Be clear and specific.** For example, SF practitioners usually begin first meetings by saying, "I'd like to take a few moments to get acquainted before we get started. It is ok if I ask you a few questions?" Once the client signals their agreement, SFT practitioners continue with questions focusing on the details of client's skills, resources, and achievements. Here are a few examples of the sorts of questions SFT practitioners typically use to invite their clients to describe their skills and competencies.

   • *Did you happen to discover anything that somehow made things better between when you scheduled this session and now?*

   • *Can you tell about some of the things that you like to do and that you are good at? How did learn to do these things? What else are you good at?*

- *What would other people say you are good at?*
- *What would your best friend say you are good at doing?*
- *What would your boss or co-workers say you are you best at in your job?*
- *What is your best subject at school?*
- *What else are you good at that you like to do?*
- *What are some of the things that you are already doing that are valuable and important to continue doing?*

In much the same spirit as the previous list, following a client's initial SF session, the SF practitioner begins subsequent sessions with

I would like to start by asking about what has somehow gotten better – even in some very small way – since last time we met, and if so, how you managed to notice it, what you did to encouraged it or what you did to make it happen?

Following this, the SFT practitioner asks about any details associated with whatever it was that contributed to making things better in some way, and asks if there was anything else that the client has discovered to be helpful, even a little bit.

Learning as much as possible about clients' already existing skills, resources, and abilities as early in the course of treatment as is respectfully possible is extremely important not only because of the positive tone this sets for the remainder of the session(s) but also because this information is essential to the solution development process. Further, beginning each session by talking about competencies establishes a positive mood that heightens its effectiveness and enhances the productivity of the entire SF process.

SF Compliments

The use of **compliments** to clients as an intervention has been an integral component of the SFT approach since its early development (Thomas, 2016). SF compliments are derived from specific things the client has talked about during SF sessions; SF compliments are typically offered during and at the conclusion of each session. SF compliments are always "evidence-based," that is derived from something specific that the client has described or done in the sessions.

SF compliments take two forms: *Direct* and *Indirect*.

Direct SF Compliments

Direct compliments are clearly stated validations designed to communicate that the SFT practitioner is appreciatively noting something positive that the client has done in general, or most typically, a behavior associated with making an effort to move toward an already specified goal. For example:

I am so impressed that you got an A on your chemistry exam, especially given how busy you have been with work, as well as caring for you daughter and taking online classes at night!

Notice that the therapist is careful to tie the compliment to specific details of real-life activities that the client is doing. In the SF approach, a well-formed direct compliment serves to provide validation, and also is a way to clearly communicate that the SF practitioner has not only been listening attentively and appreciatively but also accurately understands what the client has previously described.

When done effectively, SF direct compliments are linked to clients' real-life behavior, something they have undeniably *done* as opposed to what the practitioner personally *thinks* about them, e.g., "I think you are a really nice person" or the practitioner's personal assessment of them: "I think you are very mature for your age." A direct compliment clearly associated with a specific behavior such as achieving a high grade on an exam, completing a challenging task, exceeding what was normally expected in job performance is usually easier for someone to accept because it is based a real-life event.

When a client responds to a direct compliment by smiling and looking comfortable, SF practitioners see this as a clear indication that further direct compliments will be experienced as helpful and encouraging.

Indirect SF Compliments

Although some people respond well to direct compliments, many others do not. This is most likely to be true if they were raised in a culture where people were expected to be very modest about personal accomplishments, or if they experienced shaming or bullying by fellow students, family members, co-workers, etc., whose accomplishments they surpassed. **Indirect Compliments**, are questions that require the client to say something appreciative about themselves in order to answer (Berg & Dolan, 2001, p. 73), for example:

- *How did you manage to get such a high grade in your class?*
- *How did you figure out how to do that?*
- *How did you discover such a useful and creative idea?*

An interesting outcome of indirect compliments delivered in question form is that they usually result in the recipient making a self-validating statement in order to answer the question, for example:

> *I think I probably got a good grade on the test because I studied really hard ahead of time and didn't wait until the last minute to prepare. I also paid close attention in class and took notes.*

There are also a number of *non-verbal* versions of SF indirect compliments. For example, the late Steve de Shazer would sometimes offer a congratulatory handshake after someone described an accomplishment such as getting a job or succeeding with some particular goal. And the late Luc Isebaert, a solution-focused neuro-psychiatrist in Brugge, Belgium, sometimes utilised a little humor to indirectly compliment particularly reticent people, for example:

> *I know (from our past meetings) how much you dislike being congratulated – or even asked about – an important accomplishment. Therefore, even though I really want to compliment you, I am going to resist the temptation to tell you the big compliment that I have in my mind right now.* (Luc always had a twinkle in his eye when delivering this unique form of indirect compliment which never failed to elicit a smile from the recipient.)

SF "Experiment" Invitations

Solution-Focused Therapy practitioners typically refrain from asking clients to do assigned "homework,' which is common in many other psychotherapy approaches. However, they sometimes offer clients an optional "experiment" (de Shazer et al., 2007, pp. 11–12). Here are a few examples:

- *Between now and next time we meet, I invite you to – whenever you happen to think about it or feel like it – take a moment to pay attention to anything that you or anyone else is doing that somehow helps you helps you move in the direction of your goal.*

- *Between now and next time we meet, I would like to invite you to experiment with creating a list of things that you are already doing that are helpful and would be important to continue.*
- *Between now and next time we meet, I invite you to experiment with increasing the number of times you allow yourself to do the things that you have so far found to be helpful.*

Typically used less frequently than most other SF techniques, SF experiments are usually offered to clients as a way to support or maintain ongoing progress in between sessions. In the event that a client reports that they "forgot" to do a SF experiment or for some reason decided not to do it, the SF practitioner either assumes that the client had a good reason and moves on or asks them whether they perhaps did something else that proved useful.

SF Questions

The traditional function of asking questions in counseling is to gather information, but solution-focused practitioners typically employ questions as *interventions* (Richmond et al., 2014). SF practitioners certainly ask questions for the purpose of getting to know their clients. However, questions are also used as a way to join with them, negotiate clear goals that reflect their clients' best hopes, identify exceptions, strengths and resources, navigate SF scales, and ultimately co-develop achievable real-life solutions that their clients can readily embrace and sustain. In addition to those described already, SF questions usually are also used as the vehicle for these interventions:

Pre-session Change Question

In most problem-focused approaches it is common to ask some version of the question "What brings you here today"? While certainly reasonable to ask, SF practitioners are acutely aware that this seemingly benign initial question can set in motion a problem-oriented discussion from which it can be difficult to extricate. The pre-session change question can help practitioners and their clients identify existing things that have already proven helpful in some way, and in doing so start the process of solution-building from the beginning. The pre-session change question is usually offered early on during an initial session, but is sometimes also asked in follow-up sessions.

> *Sometimes in between scheduling an appointment and coming in, something happens that somehow helps things get better. Did anything like that happen with regard to the problem that originally caused you to schedule this appointment?*

The pre-session change question helps to ensure that already existing resources and exceptions occurring prior to or between sessions are not inadvertently overlooked; they are oftentimes incorporated into the solution development process. This question also communicates the assumption that change *could* have happened already, implying that it is an ongoing phenomenon within the reach of the client (Richmond et al., 2014).

Goal Development Questions

As soon as respectfully possible, after getting acquainted and joining with their clients, SF practitioners begin asking goal development questions. As its name suggests, the function of an SF goal development question is to develop a clear description of what the client wants to achieve as a result of coming to see the SF practitioner. This is typically generated through one or more of the following types of questions:

- *What needs to happen as a result of our meeting today in order for you (and/or the person who referred you) to be able to say afterwards that it had been a good idea to come here?*
- *What needs to happen as a result of this session in order for you to be able to honestly say afterwards that coming here was not a waste of your time?*
- *Assuming that our session is helpful today, what differences would someone who cares about you (your best friend, partner, relative, etc.) notice after our session that would indicate to them that things have gotten better for you in some way?*
- *What would indicate to the person who referred you that this session has been helpful?*

"Instead" Questions

People often initially define their goals by describing what they *do not* want, for example "*I wouldn't be working at a job I hate.*" SF practitioners use "instead" questions to respectfully shift the focus from what clients *do not* want to what they *do* want, thereby generating a clearer, more proactive and more positive goal description. For example:

> Let's suppose you are no longer working at a job that you hate. What would you like to be doing **instead**?

> You said that you want to stop constantly arguing with each other. What would you like to be doing together **instead**?

Conceptualising goals in this way reveals key details associated with clients' desired changes, ultimately making them readily accessible.

Coping Questions

Coping questions allow SF practitioners and their clients to generate useful ideas about how to best deal with difficult ongoing situations that cannot be changed such as ongoing illness, loss, the necessity of caring for a loved one suffering from dementia. Well-constructed coping questions are deliberately worded to acknowledge the difficulty of situation while gently focusing on existing and potential resources and strengths.

In instances involving challenging ongoing situations, SFT practitioners typically offer one or more versions of the following questions:

> Are there things that you have previously found helpful to prevent things from becoming even more difficult?

> What do you need to continue doing in order to prevent things from getting worse?

> Is there anything that you or someone else could do that might somehow make the situation even a little bit more bearable?

> Is there anything that you or someone else could do that might somehow make this medical condition less physically restrictive for you?

> What has helped you some how somehow find a way to carry on despite this terrible loss?

Difference Questions

Difference questions serve to help clients and SF practitioners evaluate whether a proposed behavior is likely to prove helpful and also to help generate motivation.

> What difference will that make for you?

> How will that be helpful?

What differences might other people notice that would indicate that things are going better for you?

Exception Questions

In contrast to most other approaches, SF practices emphasise the importance of exceptions, e.g., instances when the problem is not happening, happening less, or has been somehow become less troubling. Exceptions play a core role in the solution development process in which SFT practitioners collaborate with their clients to discover ways to fulfill client goals. Exception questions essential to the SFT approach and the solution development process in general. Here are a few examples:

Are there times when the problem doesn't happen or happens to a lesser degree?

What is different about the times when the problem is not happening or is happening less?

What are you (or others) doing differently when the problem is not happening or happening less?

What were you (or others) doing differently at times in the past when the problem as not happening?

SF Scaling Questions

Scaling questions allow SFT practitioners and their clients to measure the distance incrementally between clients' current position and their desired goals. It is important to note that in order for a SFT scaling question to be meaningful, it is necessary for clients to have identified a goal.[2] Once a goal has been identified, SFT practitioners utilise scaling questions to assess clients' current distance from any given goal, measure clients progress, and identify the specific steps needed in order to fulfill the clients best hopes and goals.

SFT scales should not be confused with the Pain Scales,[3] typically used in medical settings; they are significantly different. Unlike pain

---

[2]See Goal Development Questions in earlier section of this chapter. Like hopes, SFT goals need to have a reality basis in order to function in a useful and meaningful way.

[3]If you go to a hospital emergency room with a broken arm, you will likely be asked to use a Pain Scale to indicate how much pain you are currently experiencing with 0 representing "No pain" and 1–10 progressively representing higher and higher degrees pain.

scales, in which 10 represents extreme pain and 0 usually signify no pain or minimal pain, SFT scales typically use 10 to represent the goals associated with clients' best hopes regarding any given goal with 0 representing the opposite, with the numbers in between representing progressive levels of movement in the direction of the goal.

0 ———————————————————————————— 10

Because the "10" on a typical SFT scales typically represents goals derived from clients' best hopes, effective SFT scaling questions are typically reality based. To best understand this, it is helpful to note an important difference between people's *hopes* and their *wishes*: While people understandably sometimes do *wish* for things that they know to be logically impossible, it is far more useful to develop a goal based on a doable *hope*.

For example, a bereaved person might wish that their deceased loved one were still alive, that a terrorist attack or natural disaster had never happened, or that they had not suffered the physical loss of an arm or a leg. But these sorts of wishes are very different than hopes because one can only reasonably hope for something that potentially exists within the realm of everyday reality. The previous distinction exemplifies of the careful attention to language that is needed in order to effectively utilise SFT Scaling questions and the SFT approach in general.

While there are many examples of SFT scaling questions, most are based on some version of the following examples:

Imagine a scale of 0–10 in which 10 represented the problem being gone and 0 just the opposite, where are you now?

What makes it that number and not a a slightly lower number?

What are some of the things that you are you currently doing that would be important for you to continue in order to maintain your current position (number) on the scale?

What would you need to do in order to move up a point further in the director of the goal?

Let's suppose that you suddenly moved up a point on the scale, what would you find yourself doing differently?

What would you need to do (or do more of) in order to move up a point on the scale?

Scaling Questions will be explored in further detail in subsequent chapters.

The Miracle Question

The SFT Miracle Question was originally created by Insoo Kim Berg in response to a sad, beleaguered woman who, when asked what would help, responded that "it would take a miracle" in order for her to be able to deal with her situation. Touched by the woman's extreme distress and not knowing what else to offer, Insoo asked her to describe what would be different if a miracle really did happen and the problems were suddenly resolved. Here is an example of the SFT Miracle Question:

> *Let's suppose that sometime tonight while you were sleeping, a sort of miracle happens and suddenly the problem that brought you here is gone. But because you were sleeping when this very special kind of miracle happened, you wouldn't know that anything had changed until you woke up and started going through your day. What would be the first small thing you would notice that was different after you woke up and started going through your day?*

Not surprisingly, clients typically fall silent for several seconds after being asked the SFT Miracle Question; experienced SFT practitioners recognise this momentary silence as a signal that clients are taking a moment to think. Similarly some clients begin their answer with "I don't know ..." before pausing again for a few seconds and eventually continuing to answer the question.

This common initial reaction to the SFT Miracle Question is not surprising given that answering the question entails imagining a dramatically different alternative version of everyday reality in which they awaken one morning and discover that their life has been transformed in significant ways.

Once their clients begin the process of answering the Miracle Question, SF practitioners listen attentively until they finish speaking. At this point, they usually ask a series of additional questions in order to generate a highly detailed description of what will be different after the miracle happens and the problem is gone. Here are a few examples of these sorts of questions:

> *What else would you notice that is different after the miracle?*
>
> *What differences will other people in your life (partners, close friends, children, co-workers, bosses, pets etc) notice in the way you behave after the miracle has happened?*
>
> *What else?*

This process continues until a richly detailed description focusing on all the big and small behavioral changes that characterise life after the miracle has been elicited from the client.

Constructing Solutions Using Exceptions, Scaling, Instead Questions, and the Miracle Question

SFT practitioners variously utilise all of the techniques described in this section to collaborate with their clients to co-develop a practical real-life solution to the issue for which the client seeks help. While we will explore this process in far greater detail in subsequent chapters, for now it can be summarised as follows: Once clients identify a goal, SFT practitioners use "instead" questions and/or the miracle question to generate a detailed description of how the client's everyday life and behavior will be different when the goal or "miracle" they envisioned has been achieved. They then work *backwards*, utilising exception questions and scaling questions to discover the resources already present in the client's everyday life to generate practical, sustainable solutions.

SFT and Hybrid Versions of the Approach

SF is a goal-focused, evidence-based approach that collaboratively utilises specific techniques to develop solutions by utilising resources (e.g., *exceptions*) to fulfill client goals. This book reflects the official version of SF described in the official Solution-Focused Brief Therapy Treatment Manual (Solution-Focused Brief Therapy Association 2013; Trepper et al., 2012) upon which the research evidence in support of SF practices is based.

In order to accurately understand what it means to utilise the SF approach, it is helpful to make a distinction between hybrid approaches that incorporate some SF techniques into a pre-existing model, and the actual evidence-based SF approach. While it is doubtlessly possible to incorporate some techniques from other treatment models into an overall SF approach, the converse is not necessarily true. For example, approaches that require an expert stance on the part of the therapist are not compatible with the SFBT approach (de Shazer et al., 2021, p. 160). So, for instance, a psychotherapy model integrating psychodynamic therapy and SFT would *not* be considered SFT since it would violate the cardinal SF tenet that the client is the expert in their own lives, and thus solution-building needs to be constructed collaboratively.

This does not mean that there are not ways to use some aspects of other evidence-based intervention models. In fact, de Shazer et al. (2021, p. 160) have identified three ways that SF and other practices currently co-exist.

In the evidence-based version, SF practitioners exclusively utilise the core SFT assumptions and techniques. For example, the practitioner and client equally share the expert role by working collaboratively to develop unique solutions that fulfill the client's goals, SF scaling is used in most sessions, etc.

In the expanded evidenced-based version, SF assumptions and tenets inform not only the overall practice approach but also how the entire agency, school, or businesses is run. This might include using the SF approach in employee supervision, customer support, and overall organisational management.

Lastly, a hybrid version involves incorporating some SF techniques while primarily utilising a different approach. For example, a Cognitive-Behavioral therapist might respond to a client's description of a good week in a solution-focused manner by exploring what the client did that was helpful in making it a good week. But he would likely also ask about whether the client utilised the CBT skills taught in the previous session, thereby maintaining the expert role. The same is true for EMDR and other therapies in which the professional instructs or directs the client, thereby determining the course of sessions.

For the sake of brevity, the material in this book solely reflects the evidence-based versions. This is not intended to imply criticism of hybrid intervention models. There are many "right" ways to implement positive change and all deserve to be viewed appreciatively and respectfully.

RESEARCH ON SFT

SFT is an *evidence-based* approach to counseling and psychotherapy (Kim et al., 2010; 2019). There have been over 200 empirical research studies on the SFT, the majority of which have taken place over the past 15 years (Solution-Focused Brief Therapy Association, 2023). The conclusion of eight meta-analyses, a number of systematic reviews, and the assessment based on the most recent scholarly research is that SFT is an effective approach for the treatment of psychological problems, with outcomes similar to or better than other evidenced-based approaches, such as Cognitive Behavior Therapy (CBT) and Interpersonal Therapy (IT), but that these outcomes are found with fewer sessions using an approach style that is more benign to the client (Gingerich et al., 2012; Iveson, 2002; Kim et al., 2010; Kim et al., 2019; Trepper & Franklin, 2012). As a result, SFT is increasingly being used around the world as a primary approach for the treatment of psychological, behavioral, and relational problems.

SFT has been shown to be effective for a wide range of problems, for example, child behavioral problems such as conduct disorder (Kim, 2008); improving parenting skills (e.g., Carr et al., 2017); substance use disorders (Kim et al., 2018; Smock et al., 2008); depression (Gingerich and Peterson, 2013); anxiety (e.g., Schmit & Schmit, 2016); and domestic violence (McCollum et al., 2011). In addition, SFT has been shown to be effective in health and medical settings (Zhang et al., 2018); schools (e.g., Wallace et al., 2020); foster care adjustment (e.g., Pakrosnis & Čepukienė, 2012); social service agencies (e.g., Antle et al., 2012); organisational management (McKergow, 2012); and life-coaching (e.g., Grant, 2017)

As is evidenced by its vast use and influence, SF practices can be considered not just a model of counseling and psychotherapy but also a major organising approach to human relations.

CHAPTER SUMMARY

SFT is a short-term, goal-focused, evidence-based approach to helping individuals, couples, families, businesses, social institutions, and organisations formulate, achieve and maintain positive change. The approach was developed in the late 1980s by Insoo Kim Berg, Steve de Shazer and their team of colleagues and students at the Milwaukee Brief Family Therapy Center. Unlike most other therapeutic approaches which are primarily theory-driven and most often developed in academic settings, SFT was developed inductively, based directly on carefully and repeatedly observing what worked most effectively with an inner city clinic clientele seeking help with a wide range of problems including substance misuse, family and couple issues, homelessness, depression, anxiety, and other issues. A set of unique, highly practical techniques serve as the primary vehicle for implementing SFT in a variety of settings including mental health, social services, healthcare, schools, volunteer organisations, business coaching, and self-help.

SFT sessions tend to be positive in tone, focusing on developing practical solutions rather than excavating the history of clients' problems. Extensive research has shown SFT to require less time to achieve the same level of effectiveness as other therapy approaches such as Cognitive Behavioral Therapy and Interpersonal Therapy.

EXPERIENTIAL SF EXERCISE

This optional exercise is designed to provide a direct personal experience of the resource appreciative way of thinking that characterises the SF approach:

> Give someone you are close to a SF Direct Compliment and give another person in your life (perhaps even the same person) an SF Indirect Compliment. Notice how they react. (You could also try imagining how you would personally react if someone gave you a Direct or Indirect SF Compliment. Are you a person who would likely react most positively to a direct or an indirect SF compliment?)

REFERENCES

Antle, B. F., Christensen, D. N., Van Zyl, M. A., & Barbee, A. P. (2012). The impact of the Solution based casework (SBC) practice model on federal outcomes in public child welfare. *Child Abuse & Neglect*, *36*(4), 342–353.

Bannink, F. P. (2008). Solution focused mediation. *Conflict Resolution Quarterly*, *25*(2), 163–183.

Berg, I. K., & Dolan, Y. (2001). *Tales of solutions: A collection of hope-inspiring stories*. New York: WW Norton & Co.

Carr, A., Hartnett, D., Brosnan, E., & Sharry, J. (2017). Parents plus systemic, solution-focused parent training programs: Description, review of the evidence base, and meta-analysis. *Family Process*, *56*(3), 652–668.

de Shazer, S., Dolan, Y., Korman, H., Trepper, T. S., McCollum, E. E., & Berg, I. K. (2007). *More than miracles: The state of the art of solution-focused brief therapy, 1st Ed.* New York: Routledge.

de Shazer, S., Dolan, Y., Korman, H., Trepper, T. S., McCollum, E. E., & Berg, I. K. (2021). *More than miracles: The state of the art of solution-focused brief therapy, 2nd Ed.* New York: Routledge.

Gingerich, W. J., Kim, J. S., & MacDonald, A. J. (2012). Solution-Focused Brief Therapy outcome research. In Cynthia Franklin, Terry S. Trepper, Wallace J. Gingerich, & Eric E. McCollum (Eds.), *Solution-focused brief therapy: A handbook of evidence-based practice*. New York: Oxford University Press, pp. 95–111.

Gingerich, W. J., & Peterson, L. T. (2013). Effectiveness of solution-focused brief therapy: A systematic qualitative review of controlled outcome studies. *Research on Social Work Practice*, *23*(3), 266–283.

Grant, A. M. (2017). Solution-focused cognitive-behavioral coaching for sustainable high performance and circumventing stress, fatigue, and burnout. *Consulting Psychology Journal: Practice and Research*, *69*(2), 98–111.

Iveson, C. (2002). Solution-focused brief therapy. *Advances in Psychiatric Treatment*, *8*, 149–157.

Kim, J. S. (2008). Examining the effectiveness of solution-focused brief therapy: A meta-analysis. *Research on Social Work Practice, 18*, 107–116.

Kim, J. S., Brook, J., & Akin, B. A. (2018). Solution-focused brief therapy with substance-using individuals: A randomized controlled trial study. *Research on Social Work Practice, 28*(4), 452–462.

Kim, J. S., Brook, J. W., Liming, K., Park, I. Y., Akin, B. A., & Franklin, C. (2022). Randomized controlled trial study examining positive emotions and hope in solution-focused brief therapy with substance using parents involved in child welfare system. *International Journal of Systemic Therapy*, 1–21.

Kim, J., Jordan, S. S., Franklin, C., Froerer, A. (2019). Is solution-focused brief therapy evidence-based? An update 10 years later. *Families in Society: The Journal of Contemporary Social Services, 100*, 1–12.

Kim, J. S., Smock, S., Trepper, T., McCollum, E., & Franklin, C. (2010). Is solution-focused brief therapy evidence-based? *Families in Society: The Journal of Contemporary Social Services, 91*, 3894–4009.

Lipchik, E., Derks, J, LaCourt, M., & Nunnally, E. (2012). The evolution of solution-focused brief therapy. In Cynthia Franklin, Terry S. Trepper, Wallace J. Gingerich, & Eric E. McCollum (Eds.), *Solution-focused brief therapy: A handbook of evidence-based practice*. New York: Oxford University Press, pp. 3–19.

McKergow, M. (2012). Solution-focused approaches in management. In Cynthia Franklin, Terry S. Trepper, Wallace J. Gingerich, & Eric E. McCollum (Eds.), *Solution-focused brief therapy: A handbook of evidence-based practice*. New York: Oxford University Press, pp. 327–341.

McCollum, Eric E., Stith, Sandra M., & Thomsen, Cynthia J. (2011). Solution-focused brief therapy in the conjoint couples treatment of intimate partner violence. In Cynthia J., Franklin, Terry S., Trepper, Wallace J., Gingerich, & Eric E., McCollum (Eds.), *Solution-focused brief therapy: A handbook of evidence-based therapy*. New York: Oxford University Press, pp. 183–195.

Pakrosnis, R., & Čepukiené, V (2012). Outcomes of solution-focused brief therapy for adolescents infester care and health care settings. In Cynthia Franklin, Terry S. Trepper, Wallace J. Gingerich, & Eric E. McCollum (Eds.), *Solution-focused brief therapy: A handbook of evidence-based practice*. New York: Oxford University Press, pp. 299–326.

Panichelli, C. (2013). Humor, joining, and reframing in psychotherapy: Resolving the auto-double-bind. *The American Journal of Family Therapy, 41*(5), 437–451.

Richmond, C. J., Jordan, S. S., Bischof, G. H., & Sauer, E. M. (2014). Effects of solution-focused versus problem-focused intake questions on pre-treatment change. *Journal of Systemic Therapies, 33*(1), 33.

Schmit, E. L., Schmit, M. K., & Lenz, A. S. (2016). Meta-analysis of solution-focused brief therapy for treating symptoms of internalizing disorders. *Counseling Outcome Research and Evaluation, 7*(1), 21–39.

Smock, S. A., Trepper, T. S., Wetchler, J. L., McCollum, E. E., Ray, R., & Pierce, K. (2008). Solution-focused group therapy for level 1 substance abusers. *Journal of Marital and Family Therapy, 34*, 107–120.

Solution-Focused Brief Therapy Association (2013). *Solution-focused Therapy treatment manual for working with individuals, 2nd Version.* https://www.sfbta.org/wp-content/uploads/2022/04/SFBT_Revised_Treatment_Manual_2013.pdf.

Solution-Focused Brief Therapy Association (2023). *Current SFBT research.* https://www.sfbta.org/activities/current/.

Thomas, F. (2016). Complimenting in solution-focused brief therapy. *Journal of Solution-Focused Practices, 2*(1), 3.

Trepper, T. S., Dolan, Y., McCollum, E. E., & Nelson, T. (2006). Steve De Shazer and the future of solution-focused therapy. *Journal of Marital and Family Therapy, 32*(2), 133–139.

Trepper, T. S., & Franklin, C. (2012). The future of research in solution-focused brief therapy. In Cynthia Franklin, Terry S. Trepper, Wallace J. Gingerich, & Eric E. McCollum (Eds.), *Solution-focused brief therapy: A handbook of evidence-based practice.* New York: Oxford University Press, pp. 405–412.

Trepper, T. S., McCollum, E., De Jong, P., Korman, H., Gingerich, W., & Franklin, C. (2012). Solution-focused therapy treatment manual for working with individuals. In Cynthia Franklin, Terry S. Trepper, Wallace J. Gingerich, & Eric E. McCollum (Eds.), *Solution-Focused Brief Therapy: A handbook of evidence-based practice.* New York: Oxford University Press, 20–36.

Wallace, L. B., Hai, A. H., & Franklin, C. (2020). An evaluation of working on what works (WOWW): A solution-focused intervention for schools. *Journal of Marital and Family Therapy, 46*(4), 687–700.

Zhang, A., Franklin, C., Currin-McCulloch, J., Park, S., & Kim, J. (2018). The effectiveness of strength-based, solution-focused brief therapy in medical settings: A systematic review and meta-analysis of randomized controlled trials. *Journal of Behavioral Medicine, 41*, 139–151.

2

WHAT SOLUTION-FOCUSED PRACTITIONERS DO AND DO NOT DO

Key Assumptions

This chapter presents the assumptions that distinguish SFT practices from other psychotherapy and problem-solving approaches, and which allows SF conversations to function in its unique way. These key assumptions are illustrated with case examples and discussions which will exemplify their use in practice. This is followed by a Chapter Summary, a Glossary of Key Terms, and an Experiential Exercise designed to demonstrate how embracing an SF assumption can influence how people perceive and potentially respond to others' behavior in real-life contexts. For the purpose of clarity, this chapter will focus on solution-focused *therapy*, but the underlying assumptions apply to all forms of SF practice.

WHY ASSUMPTIONS MATTER

In order to appreciate the importance of the assumptions that inform the SF approach, it is helpful to remember that most traditional psychotherapy approaches are based on very different assumptions (Bannink, 2007), specifically:

1. The professional is the expert.
2. Solutions are necessarily directly related to the cause of the client's problem(s).

DOI: 10.4324/9781003401230-2

3. Treatment cannot begin until the practitioner has completed an extensive history, carefully examined every detail of the client's problem(s), and assigned a diagnosis.

In contrast to SFT where treatment begins with the first session, and usually requires five sessions or less (Kim et al., 2019; Trepper & Franklin, 2012), approaches based on the previous assumptions can easily entail months or years. Furthermore, treatment based on problem-focused psychotherapy usually begins after a lengthy evaluation process entailing multiple sessions dedicated to exploring all historical details and symptomatology associated with the clients' problem, ruling out a variety of potential causes, and developing a diagnosis.

If at this point you are beginning to sense that the SF approach is radically different from most other psychotherapy models, you are absolutely right! As you might expect, the set of unique assumptions that comprise the basis for SFT differ from those of more traditional approaches in significant ways. We will now explore the assumptions that inform the SF approach and examine how they impact the way SF practitioners view and interact with their clients.

A FIRST-HAND ACCOUNT OF SFT ASSUMPTIONS IN ACTION

To illustrate how SF assumptions can affect the lives of real people on a day-to-day basis, I will describe how they impacted my work with traumatised adolescents early as a young psychotherapist at a residential shelter for homeless and runaway teenagers.

The majority of the teenagers who came to the shelter were escaping chaotic living environments characterised by severe neglect, food insecurity, and in many cases, horrific physical, emotional, and sexual abuse. Many had been abandoned by caregivers or biological parents who had variously gone missing, were incarcerated, or rendered incapable of functioning by severe mental illness exacerbated by ongoing substance addiction; some of the teens had been forced into prostitution by adult family members to finance the latter's drug addiction.

Not surprisingly, given what they had endured, most of the kids staying at the shelter were experiencing post-traumatic stress symptoms: Nightmares, flashbacks, concentration difficulties, depression, anxiety, insomnia, and they found it difficult to trust most adults. Nighttime was oftentimes especially difficult for them. Many had trouble getting to sleep or sleeping through the night and some deliberately tried to avoid going to sleep in an attempt to avoid terrifying recurring nightmares associated with traumatic experiences.

The shelter staff was expected to follow a traditional psycho-therapy approach (described at the beginning of this chapter) based on assumptions that experts always knew best and that the best way to "help" people heal from traumatic experiences was to require them to describe all the details of every horrific experience they had endured, explore and express every painful emotion associated with those experience, and finally offer them various coping strategies to help with a variety of post-traumatic symp-toms a which had typically worsened after focusing on their traumatic experiences.

This treatment approach was based on the widely accepted but unproven theoretical assumption that disturbing memories, emo-tions, and images associated with traumatic experiences were akin to a pressurised tube of toxic material that needed to be repeatedly opened up and released until it had been emptied.

Perhaps not surprisingly, the kids at the shelter categorically rejected the idea that revisiting any of the painful life experiences they had endured could prove helpful:

> I've already talked to someone at Social Services about what happened – that's how I ended up here in the shelter, they protested.

> Talking about it (traumatic experiences) in group just brings all the bad things that happened into my mind again and afterwards I feel a lot worse.

> After I talk about it my mind keeps going back there, I can't stop thinking about it, and I have nightmares afterwards.

In addition to nightmares and sleep disturbance, they described a variety of other symptoms including worsening gastronomical issues, and concentration difficulties always worsening following any situ-ation where they were required to talk about their painful past experiences.

I was responsible for providing two daily group therapy sessions for the kids staying at the shelter Their ages ranged from 13 to 19. The morning group met immediately after breakfast and a second group met in the late afternoon. Kids currently attending classes at a local school (most were not) were allowed to miss the morning groups, but everyone was expected to attend the evening group.

Although staff was expected to get the kids to talk about their traumatic experiences, whenever the idea that it might be helpful "talk about what happened" or "tell your story" was introduced the kids responded by silently staring into space. In a group setting, the silence would eventually be followed by several kids loudly making wisecracks, others kicking the chair of the kid sitting next to them or making noises designed to simulate personal body functions.

Night-time at the shelter seemed especially difficult for many of the kids and oftentimes especially chaotic, and staff oftentimes had difficulty maintaining order. The shelter was situated in a very old building with wooden floors that registered every movement. The boys' and girls' respective dorms were situated on the second floor and separated only by a wide hallway. Although nothing in my previous training had adequately prepared me for working with these severely traumatised kids, night shifts were particularly challenging. Throughout the night kids were periodically running back and forth across the hallway despite my repeatedly pleading that they return to their beds and go to sleep.

I feared that little was being accomplished in my daily groups with the kids, and that their required attendance only served to further alienate them and deepen their distrust of adults. Searching for an alternative approach, I found a detailed article describing the essential ideas of the Solution-Focused approach being developed at the time by Steve de Shazer, Insoo Kim Berg, and their team of colleagues at the Milwaukee Brief Family Therapy Center. I was immediately impressed by how markedly different the SF assumptions were from the ones that characterized most other treatment approaches being utilised at that time and decided to start utilising the SF approach in my work.

THE KEY ASSUMPTIONS THAT INFORM THE SFT APPROACH

Here is a listing of the key assumptions that inform the SF approach (Solution-Focused Brief Therapy Association, 2013), along with a description and an example of how the assumptions were applied in the teenage runaway program described previously:

- *Clients are the ultimate experts on their own lives and what is needed in order for their lives to get better.*
- *SF practitioners are the experts on which questions to ask in order to co-construct practical, sustainable real-life solutions with their clients.*

- *No problem happens all the time; there are always exceptions that can be utilised.*
- *Small steps can lead to large changes.*
- *The future is both created and negotiable.*
- *Clients have a good reason for the ways that they think and behave.*

Clients Are the Ultimate Experts on Their Own Lives and What Is Needed in Order for Their Lives to Get Better

Unlike practitioners of most other psychotherapy approaches, SF practitioners view their clients as possessing significant expertise.

In order to apply the above assumption to my groups at the shelter, it was important that I ask the residents what would be most helpful for *them* to talk about that day and what goals it would be helpful for each of *them* to focus on. This did not mean that I was no longer responsible for what happened in groups or individual sessions; it only meant that I needed to respect what the residents said was important to them in terms of meeting their goals.

Not surprisingly, clients are typically more invested and willing to implement solutions derived from their own unique and highly personalised expert descriptions of what they need. Inevitably, they are the people best equipped to describe what will tell them that things have gotten better, and what needs to continue in order to sustain the changes that serve to make things better. And ultimately, they are the ones best equipped to identify the specifics of what it will ultimately take to motivate themselves to continue moving forward.

SF Practitioners Are the Experts on Which Questions to Ask in Order to Co-Construct Practical, Sustainable Real-Life Solutions with Their Clients

SF practitioners are responsible for the manner in which SF sessions are conducted. They are expected to know which questions to ask in order to help their clients generate a description of what will be different when the problem for which they are seeking help is gone or resolved, collaborate with their clients to develop clear, proactive goals based upon that description, and co-create a tenable real-life plan for achieving them.

While some people might find it difficult to imagine that asking questions to a group of unruly teenagers would result in them coming up with practical ideas about what would be most immediately helpful to them in the aftermath of severe complex trauma the residents demonstrated an impressive ability to do exactly that when they were if asked the right questions, for example:

> *What do we need to focus on today in order for you to be able to honestly say afterwards that coming to group today was helpful and not a waste of your time?*

Although this question had to be repeated several times before the residents responded, their answers were frequently highly practical, realistic, and insightful and ultimately resulted in goals that both they and the staff could readily embrace:

> *We need to talk about something that makes us feel better, not something that brings us down or will give us bad dreams tonight.*
>
> *We need to talk about something practical that we can do to make things better.*
>
> *We need to come up with ideas for what we can do or where we can go when we leave this shelter; we need to figure out what might be possible?*
>
> *We need to figure out a way that the kids who want to sleep at night don't keep getting woken up by the kids who don't want to sleep.*
>
> *We need to stop kicking each other in group.*
>
> *I need to get in touch with my aunt (uncle, sibling, extended family, significant other, etc).*
>
> *I afraid I'm going to start using (drugs) again. I need to figure out a place to stay after I leave here where people are not dealing or using (drugs).*
>
> *I need to get a phone number to contact my probation officer.*
>
> *Some of us need to shut up for a few minutes in group sometimes so other people can talk too.*
>
> *I can't go home because my mother's boyfriend keeps beating her and I am afraid that if I go back there I will lose control and kill him and end up in jail. I need to find a place where I can stay while I try to finish high school.*
>
> *I need to learn job skills.*

No Problem Happens All the Time; There Are Always Exceptions That Can Be Utilised

This SF assumption highlights a concept often overlooked in problem-focused approaches. It empowers SF practitioners and their clients to search for *exceptions* to a problem in the form of useful and/or adaptive healthy behaviors that already exist at least to some degree within the client's everyday repertoire. Exceptions constitute a powerful resource for SF practitioners and their clients because they emanate from the client and, because they have already occurred, are more likely to continue. Exceptions are the most essential ingredient needed to generate sustainable real-life solutions and coping strategies that clients can readily embrace.

Even after enduring extremely adversarial ongoing life situations like those being endured by many of the teens staying at the shelter, no problem happens to the same degree at every moment in the day or night. There are always some moments when things are somehow a little bit better, more bearable, safer or slightly less difficult. Identifying and exploring the details of an exception, e.g. a time when the problem does not happen or happens less, opens the possibility of replicating it to generate an effective, sustainable solution. Sometimes focusing on even a small exception has the capacity to kindle a flicker of hope, or at least introduce a little bit of movement in the direction of hope.

The key assumption that no problem happens all the time led me to ask questions that eventually resulted in serious discussions with the teens about what might be done to improve their nighttime experience at the shelter. As noted, nights had typically been an especially difficult time for the residents and consequently very challenging for the staff. Many of the teens suffered from nighttime anxiety and depression, flashbacks, and nightmares associated with the abuse they had suffered. Nevertheless, some nights had definitely been better than others.

Focusing on these exceptions – nights when they had somehow managed to sleep better, suffered fewer nightmares, managed to wake up in a more hopeful or at least more positive frame of mind – generated numerous ideas about how nighttimes could be improved. Several described that they slept better and seemed less likely to have nightmares if they avoided watching scary movies before going to sleep. Others identified that listening to relaxing music before going to sleep helped, as did focusing evening groups that focused on generating positive plans for the next day. The plans could involve something very simple: A small group outing or field trip, an anticipated television program or movie, planning a visit with a caring family member, older cousin or sibling, or making an appointment with a supportive community worker, guidance counselor, or teacher.

Following a series of detailed discussions and brainstorming sessions about what might lead to better sleep and more restful nights, a number of residents began reaching out to staff individually for help. They asked if it would be okay to come downstairs and talk things over if they felt too upset to sleep or had experienced a particularly frightening dream or flashback. Oftentimes deeply touching and revelatory, these late-night conversations sometimes led to significant changes in a resident's general attitude and resulted in a new willingness to observe various rules involving group attendance, mealtimes, curfews, evening quiet time, and lights-out that they had previously resisted; the overall atmosphere gradually began shifting in a positive direction.

The next SF assumption reflects the overarching stance of pragmatically grounded optimism, which is at the core of the SF approach.

Small Steps Can Lead to Large Changes

Small changes can and often do result in major behavioral changes. In many cases, one small positive change can gradually instigate a long series of additional ones. And the act of identifying, envisioning, and implementing a series of small changes renders the change process more readily accessible for people who would otherwise be too hesitant or not yet sufficiently motivated to immediately address a larger, potentially more daunting goal.

For example, during an SF group discussion with the shelter residents on the topic of what might help them to find the necessary strength to try to move forward with their everyday lives in various ways, they responded that it would be helpful to reach out to people who had previously been supportive to them. This discussion led to one of the teens telephoning his former high school guidance counselor who not only encouraged him to return to school but also provided help in registering for summer school classes and a series of after-school activities scheduled to begin shortly.

For many of the residents, taking that first small step of a single phone call to a former guidance counselor, teacher, or youth pastor, initiated a series of additional small, incremental steps that gradually led to earning a high school diploma, completing classes at a local community college, and acquiring marketable job skills.

The next assumption references the future focus inherent in the SF approach.

The Future Is Both Created and Negotiable

One of the first SF questions I offered to the teens in my groups at the shelter invited them to focus directly on the future, in this case, the immediate future:

What is one small thing that you could do in the next 24 hours that would help you to move, even a tiny bit, in the direction of the way you want your life to be?

Another SF question that I frequently offered to residents who complained about various things that they did not like challenged them, to:

Describe one small thing that you could do in the next 24 hours that you like as an alternative to focusing on something you don't like? It should be something that helps you move (even a little bit) in the direction of what you want your life to be like in the future.

Although most initially responded to questions about their preferred future by describing major changes, e.g. "I want to have a new car, a place to live of my own, and a lot of spending money," repeatedly encouraging them to identify one single specific action that they could reasonably accomplish in the next 24 hours gradually led to a cogent description of small, practical, positive steps that proved to be within the teen's reach, e.g.:

I am going to get up early starting tomorrow morning so that I can make any important phone calls I need to make before morning group (or school) starts.

I am going to take a shower tonight and get some clean clothes from the shelter clothing bank, so that I start feeling better about how I look.

I'm going to check in with my probation officer this afternoon so I don't get in any more trouble; I need a clean record to get a decent job so I can save money and buy a house.

I'm going to do some laundry; I want to start taking better care of myself.

I am going to call my aunt (or other relative) so I can feel more in touch with my family, or at least the ones I want to be in touch with …

I am going to attend a meditation class at the community center. Someday, I want to teach meditation and martial arts for a living when I am older.

I am going to paint a picture tomorrow. I feel happier when I am making art; I want to be a professional artist someday.

As I continued to utilise the SF approach in my daily groups at the shelter, progressively more residents appeared to be sleeping or at least quietly resting during the night, staying in their own beds, and participating more actively in group activities and generally following the rules of the shelter. Many no longer needed to be reminded to get out of bed in the morning. Several started showing up at the breakfast table with smiles on their faces. Being asked SF questions that invited them to focus on the future, particularly the very immediate future, rather than excruciatingly painful past events, clearly had a positive impact on their ability to manage and cope with post-traumatic stress symptoms and participate in everyday life at the shelter. In the event that they would eventually feel a need to revisit painful past events, they would do so freely of their own accord rather than feeling pressured and forced.

Assuming That Clients Have a Good Reason

SF practitioners deliberately choose to assume that unless proven otherwise, their clients have a "good reason" (at least from the clients' perspective) for thinking and behaving in the way they do. If a client responds negatively to a question or appears uncooperative, SF practitioners view it as indication that what they are doing is, at least in some way, not helpful for the client at this time.

The "Good Reason" stance is markedly different from many other approaches where client's problematic or disruptive behavior would have been immediately interpreted as "resistance." Depending on various conceptualisations of "resistance," some might even suggest that a clients' pain "needed to get worse" before they would become sufficiently cooperative to get better or that their "defenses" might need to be "broken down" in order to benefit from therapy. The SF approach assumes exactly the opposite.

Did my shifting to an SF approach ultimately benefit the teens I worked with at the homeless shelter? Focusing on small, concrete goals based on each resident's stated hopes and preferences introduced a sense of hope that they could more readily embrace. The "stonewalling" (refusal to speak) and disruptive behavior ceased. More of them began sleeping through the night, staying in their respective dorms, getting up in the morning without being reminded, and increasingly showing up for breakfast with smiles on their faces. Overall, the SF emphasis on focusing proportionately more on the future than the past created a much-needed context of hope for these young people who had endured so much in their relatively short lives.

The series of examples in the previous section has highlighted several significant differences between the assumptions that inform the SFT approach and those used to inform traditional, problem-focused approaches, and illustrated how SF practitioners' use of them can impact the real-life experience of vulnerable clients.

Other Fundamental Guidelines for SF Practice

Besides the foundational assumptions just reviewed, there are also some important guidelines that all SF practice follows (Trepper et al., 2012). Those guidelines are as follows:

- *If it's not broken, don't fix it.*
- *If something is working, do more of it.*
- *If it's not working, do something different.*
- *The solution is not necessarily directly related to the problem.*
- *The language requirements for solution development are different than those needed to describe a problem.*

If It's Not Broken, Don't Fix It

This guideline often strikes people as ridiculously obvious, but its inclusion in the SF approach signals a deliberate and in some ways, even radical departure from traditional, pathology-based approaches that emphasise the importance or even the necessity of uncovering and subsequently addressing "underlying" problems for which the client did not seek help or in some cases might not personally be aware of or even regard as a problem.

Imagine, for example, that Mike decides to give up smoking. Although he has already gotten through the past two weeks without smoking, he is worried about falling back into the habit again which happened on two previous occasions. So Mike schedules an appointment with a mental health provider to get some help. Let's assume that this particular mental health provider is using a traditional addiction treatment model. The following is based on a real-life story.

During his appointment, Mike confides that he has so far found it very helpful to eat a handful of sunflower seeds whenever he has a craving for a cigarette. (This happens to be an idea that he recently read about in a popular magazine). He is pleased with the progress he has made so far, and in addition to continuing to eat an occasional handful of sunflower seeds as a substitute for smoking a cigarette, he has also promised himself an ice cream sundae if he manages to get through the weekend without smoking.

Based on his traditional addiction treatment training, Mike's therapist might, instead of complimenting his client on discovering a healthier substitute for cigarettes and encouraging him to try out the idea of further motivating himself with an ice cream sundae reward at the end of the weekend, express concern that constantly ingesting sunflower seeds could potentially turn into a new addiction, and that rewarding himself with a weekly ice cream sundae could also potentially lead to weight gain and even yet another addiction, in this case, a compulsive eating disorder. "You wouldn't want to end up replacing one addiction with another one," he points out.

Now let's contrast this with how an SF practitioner, would most likely respond to Mike's description of replacing cigarettes with sunflower seeds and planning to reward himself with a weekly ice cream sundae. The SF practitioner would start by complimenting Mike on finding a healthier replacement (a handful of sunflower seeds) for smoking a cigarette and would likely further compliment him for already figuring out at least one way to further increase his motivation by planning to reward himself with an ice cream sundae. The practitioner would also invite Mike to think of times during the past week when he would normally have smoked a cigarette and describe in detail what he had done instead. Let's suppose that Mike responded that he went outside and washed his car in an effort to distract himself from the cigarette craving. In that case, the SF practitioner might have gone on to ask, what was that like for you? Mike would have perhaps responded that, "It was hard at first because I really wanted that cigarette, but afterwards I liked that I had gotten my car washed and that felt good."

The SF practitioner would have likely concluded the session by saying something like, "I know that this is not easy, therefore I am very impressed with the changes in behavior that you have already managed to accomplish in the past week, and I think you are clearly on the right track. I would encourage you to continue to pay attention to any other useful things that you do instead of smoking that subsequently cause you to feel good afterwards, and if you want to schedule another appointment, we can further discuss this the next time you come in."

In contrast to a number of other psychotherapy approaches which assume that it is the professional rather than the client who decides what problem needs to be addressed, SFT practitioners follow the guidelines of "If it's not broken, don't fix it" by deliberately focusing on their clients' stated goal (in this case giving up smoking) rather than seeking to address additional issues that the client does not currently consider to be problematic in this case, the possibility of becoming addicted to sunflower seeds or overeating).

If Something Is Working, Do More of It

The concept of "doing more of what is working" epitomises the overall practicality and behavioral economy of the SF approach in utilising aspects of a client's life that are currently going well or have previously gone well to develop sustainable solutions.

For example, Erika, a nurse and busy single mother of three active teenagers, had recently been required to add an extra ten hours to her already fulltime weekly workload to cover a staff shortage at the local hospital. Seeking help from an SF practitioner, she described the situation that had caused her to schedule the appointment:

> My kids were always very considerate, responsible, and well-behaved in the past. Up until just recently, they were always great about doing their chores on time so that we could get dinner on the table quickly when I came home from work at the end of the day, but lately nothing seems to be getting done. I walk in the door dead tired at the end of a 10 hour workday and my house is in complete chaos. All three of my kids are sprawled out on the couch and no one is doing what they are supposed to be doing. When I ask them to get up and do their chores, they just sit there listening to their headphones, staring into their iPhones, watching TV.

Noting her description of "previously responsible and well-behaved" children who were better at listening, the SF practitioner asked Erika to describe her own behavior during previous times when things had been better, e.g. her children had done their chores when she asked them. Erika thought about this for a few seconds and then responded,

> Before, I would come home an hour earlier, get changed out of my work clothes, put on my red apron, tie my hair back with a clip and tell my kids in a friendly but no nonsense way exactly what I needed them to do in the next hour. And they would immediately get up from whatever they had been doing and get started on their chores while I did whatever other things I needed to do and also got dinner ready. But nowadays when I walk in the door, I find the three of them lounging in the living room, staring at their computers or the television or listening to music on their head phones and I can't seem to get their attention. When I ask them to do their chores, they just continue to sit there.

Intrigued by Erika's description, the SF practitioner observed,

> It sounds like your 'no-nonsense' way of communicating worked well. What do you think would happen if you did something like that again?

Erika: These days I probably look really worn out when I come home and perhaps even sound as if I am pleading with them to help rather than insisting that it is time for them them to get up off the couch and get their chores done. Maybe I could start putting on my red apron first thing when get home and start off talking to them in that no-nonsense Mom tone like I used to when I wasn't so dead tired at the end of the day. What worries me however, is what will I do if they don't pay attention to me and start doing their chores again. Then what will I do?

SF Practitioner: Since using the 'no-nonsense' Mom approach has clearly worked in the past, I wonder what this "no-nonsense" Mom in the red apron would have responded if the kids started refusing to listen and do their chores?

Erika: 'No-nonsense' Mom would have immediately picked up the TV remote control and switched it off, turned off the computer, removed my daughter's headphones, stood there until I got full their attention, and then repeated exactly what I needed them to do.

SF Practitioner: Supposing you did that, how do you think your kids would likely react?

Erika: I think it is worth a try.

Two weeks later, Erika reported that, although her children initially ignored her when she stood in front of them wearing her red apron over her work uniform and they had protested loudly when she proceeded to turn off their various electronic devices in order to get their attention, they eventually listened and managed to complete their various chores by the time she had fixed dinner. Since then they had been completing their chores on schedule.

In Erika's case, the behavioral skills necessary to create this solution (getting the children to listen and do their chores) already existed within her behavioral repertoire. The SF practice of utilising already existing behaviors to generate and maintain solutions (*If it's working, do more of it*) takes advantage of the fact that people typically find it easier to incorporate behaviors with which they are already familiar, thereby making the resulting solution easier to integrate more readily sustainable in everyday real-life situations.

If It's Not Working, Do Something Different

Perhaps the most pragmatic of all the SF guidelines, **If it's not working, do something different** immediately shifts the focus beyond the problem, for example, what is not working, and initiates the change process. *If it's not working, do something different* invites SFT practitioners and their clients to explore what the client and others will be doing differently when the problem is gone or satisfactorily resolved. This guideline is particularly helpful when people define what they want in terms of what they would *not* be doing. Focusing on what you want to do differently or *instead* of the undesired behavior is far easier and more motivating to contemplate than just trying to imagine the absence of the undesired behavior.

Let's suppose that Seth wants to stop eating food that is bad for him, and in this case he decides to see a health care professional trained in SFT.

> Seth: *I want to stop eating fast food that is bad for me*

In this situation, the SF practitioner proceeds to ask a series of questions designed to generate a description of what Seth will be doing differently when this is no longer a problem.

> SF Practitioner: *Let's imagine that you succeed in doing exactly that. What will other people in your life (family, friends, co-workers, etc.) notice you doing differently?*
> Seth: *My family will see me fixing a lunch to bring to work, and that I am suggesting that on weekends we start going to restaurants where they have healthier foods. My friends will probably notice that I am starting to spend my time a little differently.*
> SF Practitioner: *What will they see you doing when you are spending your time differently?*
> Seth: *I will start playing tennis again, and spending time outdoors. I will start feeling more confident about how I look because I will probably lose some weight, so I will start dating again.*

As Seth answers the previous questions about ***doing something different,*** he begins to generate a set of alternative mental images through which he can begin to virtually experience a selection of increasingly specific alternative possibilities that he can subsequently use to move in the direction of her goal.

> *I used to love to play tennis and golf. I will start would start playing sports again at that park I like to visit.*

> *I will be saving money by bringing my own healthy lunch to work and use the savings to buy something I have been wanting.*

> *I will start eating healthy asian wraps and udon noodles again.*

> *I will feel better about the way I looked which will give me more more confidence; maybe I will try online dating.*

"If it's not working, do something different" orients SF practitioners to the world of possibilities contained in the clients' hopes, goals, and repertoire.

The Solution Is Not Necessarily Directly Related to the Problem

This guideline is arguably the most "game-changing" of all the SF concepts. It reflects a dramatic departure from the traditional method of approaching problems that, beginning with Sigmund Freud, has characterised all traditional psychotherapy approaches.

To fully appreciate the radical **paradigmatic shift** entailed in this guideline, bear in mind that *The solution is not necessarily directly related to the problem* runs directly counter to the medical model employed by practitioners of traditional psychotherapy approaches; that is, that it is always necessary to first identify the cause of the problem in order to successfully cure or treat it.

But mental illness and interpersonal problems do not usually lend themselves to traditional methods used to detect medical conditions, for example, microscopes that can detect bacterias that cause infection, or X-ray machines that reveal the presence of cancer or a broken bone. A mental health practitioner cannot simply look into a person's head and view the various nuances of their inner psychological state in the same way that a medical doctor or laboratory technician examines a microscopic slide or an X-ray.

By inviting their clients to describe what it will be like when the problem that brought them to therapy is either gone or sufficiently resolved to no longer constitute a problem, SF practitioners invite their clients to utilise a wide range of significant resources, including those that may or may not have any direct relationship to the cause of the problem.

Consider for for example, Jean, a recently widowed woman in her 60's. Although previously very active in her community, church, and gardening club, Jean retreated deep into her grief and became increasingly isolated and depressed during the year immediately following her husband's death. Only leaving the house to attend weekly Grief Support groups at her church or to pick up a bag of groceries, she gradually stopped returning phone calls from family members and friends. When her adult children came to check on her and realised that she was spending most of her time in bed, they became increasingly worried about her. Although last's year's routine medical check-up had indicated her to be in good physical health, it seemed to her family that Jean was likely suffering from something that was more than normal grief: They feared she was becoming seriously depressed.

Finally, after much urging from her son, Jean agreed to schedule an appointment with a local mental health professional. However, while she was still on the waiting list for an appointment, something unexpected happened in Jean's life. Late one morning, just before noon, Jean, who had recently been staying in bed later and later into the day, glimpsed some movement outside her bedroom window. Putting on her glasses and robe, she went to the window and saw a small stray dog wandering around in her yard in the snow, shaking with cold and looking like he had not eaten much for several days.

Without bothering to get dressed, Jean immediately hurried to the door, coaxed the shivering little dog into her warm kitchen, and offered it something to eat and a bowl of water which it eagerly accepted. Following that, the little dog curled up in a corner of the living room. Jean then quickly dressed and went out to buy a small package of dog food, and she stopped at the local animal shelter to see if there were any listings involving a missing dog. Following that, she returned home and posted a notice in the local community newspaper in case the little dog's family might be searching for him.

Meanwhile, Jean did her best to comfort and care for the little dog. She started getting up earlier in the morning in order to let him outside. When her children next came to check on her, they found Jean already up and dressed for the day, with the dog cuddled up next to her on the couch. With apparent satisfaction, she confided to them that the little dog never seemed to want to stay outside for long; he always seemed to want to be right by her side.

After a few weeks without hearing from any possible previous owners, Jean decided to adopt the dog. She took him to the vet for a check-up, gave him a bath, and gradually began regularly taking him on walks around the neighborhood. Jean and her dog often encountered neighbors during these walks and they were occasionally invited inside for a cup of coffee.

The daily walks increased to several times a day, and Jean's son and daughter-in-law were pleasantly surprised to learn that Jean had become increasingly active, variously working on her flower beds, visiting the local library, and inviting friends to join her for coffee and early morning dog walks. When the time came for Jean's scheduled appointment with the mental health practitioner, she called her son and asked, "I hope you don't mind that I went ahead and cancelled the appointment? I truly don't need it. That little dog makes all the difference in the world for me; he gives me a reason to get out of bed every day and go outside."

Obviously, the dog had nothing to with the original cause of Jean's distress, the tragic sudden loss of her beloved husband. And the passing of time may have also contributed to her feeling better. Nevertheless, it is obvious that the solution for problems is not necessarily always directly linked to the apparent cause of the problem. Recognising this, SFT practitioners make it a point to ask their clients whether anything has happened in between appointments, or even prior to their first appointment that has somehow contributed to making things better, even in a small way. Asking in an appreciative manner about the various details of even relatively small things that somehow have contributed to making a person's life better or at least more bearable typically has a positive amplifying effect.

The Language Requirements for Solution Development Are Different Than Those Needed to Describe a Problem

This guideline orients SFT practitioners toward questions designed to help their clients generate a detailed description of how life will be different when the problem to gone.

Imagine that Jared, aged 15, has been assigned to see a probation officer after recently damaging some school property (breaking a window), and repeatedly missing school. Let's suppose that when Jared shows up for the appointment, the probation officer initiates the conversation by asking a series of questions like, "How many times did you miss school over the past three weeks" and "How many times did your teachers find it necessary to send you to the principal's office this week because you were creating a disturbance," and/or "Did you damage any additional school property since the date that you were first put on probation?"

Notice that while the previous questions served to generate further details about the scope of the problem they elicited no information about potential solutions.

Now, let's assume that the Jared's Probation Officer used an SF approach:

> *SF Probation officer: How many times did you manage to successfully attend the classes this past week?*
>
> *Jared: I managed to get to school three days out of five this past week..*
>
> *SF Probation Officer: That's two days more than last week. How did you do it?*[1]
>
> *Jared: I went to bed earlier. I had been staying up all night playing video games and sleeping all day. But this week I decided to do something different.*
>
> *SF Probation Officer: How did you decide to do that?*
>
> *Jared: I was getting bored at home, so I decided to see what was going on with my friends, so I went to bed earlier so I would wake up in time to catch the bus. Somedays I have a hard time getting myself out of bed.*
>
> *SF Probation Officer: How did you get yourself out of bed on the days you went to school? Did you have your Mom wake you up?*
>
> *Jared: No, my Mom works night shifts so she usually sleeps until noon. I set an alarm on my phone.*
>
> *SF Probation Officer: That clearly worked. What do you think it would take for you to make it to school all week?*
>
> *Jared: Going to bed earlier. And setting the alarm on my phone ... . Yesterday I forgot to set the alarm.*
>
> *SF Probation Officer: If you had set the alarm you would have made it to school?*
>
> *Jared: Yes.*
>
> *SF Probation Officer: You are a guy who knows how to use his head – you know what to do.*[2]
>
> *Jared: Thanks.*
>
> *SF Probation Officer: How many days this week did you manage to stay out of the Principal's Office?*
>
> *Jared: All five. I didn't get sent to the principal's office this week.*
>
> *SF Probation Officer: Really?* (his tone conveys slightly humorous pleasurable surprise and approval).
>
> Jared nods.

---

[1] Notice how the SF practitioner focuses on the exception – Jared going to school – and the improvement – attending two more days than the previous week – rather than limiting the focus to the missed school days.

[2] Notice that instead of focusing on the problem by emphasising the fact that Jared missed two days of school this week and asking why he did that, the SF probation officer begins to generate a solution description by focusing on the exception (getting to school three days) and reinforcing the exception the with a compliment, e.g., *you know how to use your head*.

SF Probation Officer: I realize that you couldn't have gotten sent to the Principal's Office on the days that you didn't got to school, but how did you manage to stay out of the Principal's Office on the days that you did go to school?[3]

Jared: I don't know. I guess I just decided to focus on my work.

SF Probation Officer: I see. (Conveys approval by his tone).[4] Have there been other times when you might have gotten into trouble but managed to do something different?

Jared: Yes, probably. I guess so ...

SF Probation Officer: How did you do it?

Jared: After I broke the window, I stopped hanging out on the school grounds after school and started using a different basketball court. And I tried to not make fun of teachers so much during class because it always got me in trouble.

SF Probation Officer: Getting to bed earlier at night so you can get up early enough to up in the morning and go to school, focusing on your work, staying out of the Principal's Office, using a different basket ball court – these all seem to be things that are working well for you[5]. I think you are definitely moving in the right direction. Does this sound like something you are going to be able to continue to do?

Jared: Yes, I can do that.

SF Probation Officer: I think you are definitely moving in the right direction and I am looking forward to our next meeting. (He and Jared stand and shake hands)

DISCUSSION

As you have seen in the previous case example, this SF particular guideline, *The language requirements for solution development are different than those needed to describe a problem*, carries important real-life implications for SF practitioners and their clients. Think about how different the content (and language) of this interview

---

[3]Notice that the SF probation officer focuses on *how* rather than *why* here. While asking why might generate a description of the motivation behind a behavior, *how* typically elicits specific behavioral descriptions that can be more readily used to develop a solution.

[4]This kind of indirect SF compliment, conveyed primarily through voice tone and facial expression, allows SF practitioners to politely acknowledge an exception while continuing to further generate descriptions of a potential solution in the form of possible additional exceptions.

[5]Notice how the SF probation officer carefully uses Jared's exact words to repeat the solution description that has just been generated.

would have been if instead of exploring Jared's recent exceptions to generate a solution description (getting to bed earlier and going to school more often, focusing on his work, staying out of the principal's office, using a different basketball court, etc.) the probation officer had limited the focus to further exploring the details and/or potential causes of the problem. In contrast to the oftentimes implicitly demoralising language entailed in problem descriptions, the language required to describe solutions typically introduces positive emotions and a sense of hope.

CHAPTER SUMMARY

The SF approach is informed by a unique series of assumptions and guidelines that distinguish it from other prominent original psychotherapy approaches and allows SFT conversations to function in ways that are distinctly different from most other interactions.

This chapter began by elucidating key differences between the highly practical, resource-focused assumptions that inform the SFT approach and the theory-driven pathology-based, problem-focused assumptions that characterise most traditional psychotherapy approaches. The implications of the various SF assumptions were demonstrated through a series of detailed illustrative examples derived from the author's work at a homeless shelter. The SF assumptions which inform and guide the approach variously reflect a deep respect for the unique knowledge that exists within each person. For example, *Clients are the experts on their own lives* assumes that people *have good reason* for their views and behaviors and reminds practitioners to approach solution generation with a sense of creative possibility. *The future is both created and negotiable,* offers an implicit sense of hope. *No problem happens all the time, there are always exceptions,* creates optimism as does the idea that *Small steps can lead to large changes.*

The second half of this chapter examined, demonstrated, and discussed the practical and succinct guidelines that lead to SF practitioners' implementation of the SF approach. For example, *If it's not broken don't fix it, If something is working, do more of it* and *If it is not working do something different,* moves practitioners to think "outside the box." *The solution is not necessarily related to the problem* reminds them to be attentive to language choices. And perhaps most importantly, the fact that *The language requirements for solution development are different than those needed to describe a problem* serves to remind SF

Practitioners to pay close attention to the subtle and not so subtle limitations contained various potential word choices when formulating questions to generate solution descriptions. For example, asking someone what they *will be doing differently when* they *are* a point higher on their SF scale generates a clearer and far more useful behavioral description than asking what they would *not be doing,* or *if* they *could* be a point higher. The former wording invites hope and clarity and implies desirable possibilities. But the latter introduces doubt with the words *if* and *could*. Further, asking someone what they would *not be doing* requires the person to engage in the far more difficult task of imagining and describing the absence of undesirable behavior. It is always much easier and far more productive for solution development to describe the presence of productive behaviors.

Considered as a whole, these assumptions comprise the pragmatic, linguistic and philosophical heart and soul of the SFT approach.

EXPERIENTIAL SF EXERCISE: ASSUMING A *GOOD REASON*

This exercise is designed to provide a direct personal experience of how applying a SF assumption can potentially impact the way we perceive a person:

> *Think of a relationship that you find challenging; now deliberately choose to assume that the other person has a 'good reason' (at least from their perspective) for behaving or thinking as they do. Notice how this assumption effects the way you regard this person, and how you conceptualize your interactions with them and view their behavior.*

REFERENCES

Bannink, F. P. (2007). Solution-focused brief therapy. *Journal of Contemporary Psychotherapy, 35,* 87–94.

Kim, J., Jordan, S. S., Franklin, C., & Froerer, A. (2019). Is solution-focused brief therapy evidence-based? An update 10 years later. *Families in Society: The Journal of Contemporary Social Services, 100,* 1–12.

Solution-Focused Brief Therapy Association (2013). *Solution-focused therapy treatment manual for working with individuals, 2nd Version.* https://www.sfbta.org/wp-content/uploads/2022/04/SFBT_Revised_Treatment_Manual_2013.pdf.

Trepper, T. S., & Franklin, C. (2012). The future of research in solution-focused brief therapy. In Cynthia Franklin, Terry S. Trepper, Wallace J. Gingerich, & Eric E. McCollum (Eds.), *Solution-focused brief therapy: A handbook of evidence-based practice*. New York: Oxford University Press, pp. 405–412.

Trepper, T. S., McCollum, E., De Jong, P., Korman, H., Gingerich, W., & Franklin, C. (2012). Solution-focused therapy treatment manual for working with individuals. In Cynthia Franklin, Terry S. Trepper, Wallace J. Gingerich, & Eric E. McCollum (Eds.), *Solution-focused brief therapy: A handbook of evidence-based practice*. New York: Oxford University Press, pp. 20–36.

3

WHAT DOES A SOLUTION-FOCUSED THERAPY SESSION LOOK LIKE?

Despite the core assumptions and techniques that consistently characterise its implementation, SFT is not a rigid, "one-size-fits-all" approach but a carefully nuanced one in which clients' unique goals ultimately determine how and in which order the core SF techniques are employed (Berg & Dolan, 2001, p. 12). This chapter demonstrates a typical SF session with a person seeking to return to work after enduring a difficult experience.

The various SFT techniques employed are highlighted in bold print, and supplementary footnotes appear when pertinent. As you will see in the following case typical SFT sessions are characterised by a compassionate, respectful attitude on the part of the SF Practitioner, careful attention to clients' goals, and skillful utilisation of core SF techniques to develop the solutions needed to fulfill those goals.

SF CASE EXAMPLE: PUTTING HER LIFE BACK TOGETHER[1]

The week after Erin graduated from college, she and her boyfriend moved to an apartment in a nearby city where they both

---

[1]Although this case transcript and all other case transcripts in this book are derived from a real-life SFT session, all identifying information has been carefully altered to protect client privacy.

DOI: 10.4324/9781003401230-3

had found jobs. Three years later, he received a job promotion that required him to move to a distant city and the couple moved again. Although Erin had enjoyed her job, she was sure that she would find another one in the new city. But finding a job in the new city had proven far more difficult that anticipated. And then, less than three months after the move, Erin's boyfriend abruptly announced that he had fallen in love with someone else, packed up his belongings and left. Devastated and struggling to decide what to do next, Erin scheduled a counseling appointment with an SF Practitioner. A heavy spring rain was falling outside on the day of Erin's counseling appointment.

SF Practitioner: How are you liking this weather?[2]

Erin: I keep telling myself that the flowers must be happy.

SF Practitioner: That is a lovely way to look at it. **(Direct Compliment)**.

Erin: I am trying to be positive. I am not accustomed to this much rain.

SF Practitioner: Where are you from?

Erin: I grew up on the west coast where it is a lot drier.

SF Practitioner: This must be a big change for you.

Erin: It is. That is part of why I am here.

SF Practitioner: In that case, shall we get started? (Erin nods). *What is your best hope for how this appointment could be helpful?* **(Goal Development Question)**.

Erin: I need help figuring out what to do. I left my job to move here with my boyfriend. I have only been here for three months and two weeks ago he suddenly told me he was leaving me for someone else, quickly packed up his things and moved out. I didn't see this coming. I thought that everything was fine between us. But clearly it wasn't.

SF Practitioner: What a shock for you! This must be very difficult to take in, especially since it seems to have happened so suddenly. I am so sorry to hear that you are going through this

Erin: I have been crying a lot.

SF Practitioner: Of course. I can imagine that this situation has been very painful for you, especially given how abruptly it happened and given that you only recently moved here. And you said that you need some help figuring out

---

[2]The purpose of exchanging this sort of pleasantry before starting a session is to communicate in a relaxed manner that the SF practitioner relates to them as a fellow human being, rather than just a "client."

what to do.[3] Is that what we should focus on today, figuring out what to do?[4] **(Goal Development Question).**

Erin: Yes. I have some decisions to make.

SF Practitioner: Which is the one (decision) that you think would be most helpful to focus on first? **(Goal Development Question).**

Erin: I've been looking for a job here for the past three months and now I think I may possibly have finally found one because this morning they called and asked me to come in for a third interview. Usually in my field — IT (internet technology)— a third interview means you will likely get the job.

SF Practitioner: Wow! That's great. Is the decision about whether to accept the job (assuming that you are offered it) the what we should focus on today? **(Goal Development Question).**

Erin: No, I think I have already decided to accept the job if I get it.

SF Practitioner: You are already clear on that decision. (Erica nods). It's another decision that would be most important for us to focus on today?

Erica: Yes. It's interesting ... before I came here today I thought that I should probably spend my time here talking about whether to stay in this city. But after you asked me what would be most important to focus on, I realised that it's really not about the city or even whether to stay in my current apartment. I am really sad about the way my boyfriend ended our relationship, but I don't want to let that defeat me. If and when I decide to leave this city, I want it to be on my own terms and my own decision; I don't want to sneak out the back door, return to my home town and live with my parents while I try to put my life back together. I want to decide how to put my life back together on my own terms, so that if at some point I do decide to leave, I will be leaving by the front door, not the back door.[5]

SF Practitioner: You are clear that you want to put your life together on your own terms in a way that would leave you free to stay or leave depending on what you decided. Is that accurate? (Client nods). Is that the goal we should focus on today: Figuring out how to put your life back together in the best way for you?

---

[3]Notice how the SF practitioner acknowledges the client's feelings and expresses compassion, and then immediately seeks to clarify her understanding of the client's goal for the session. In the event that the client had expressed a need to focus further on her feelings rather than the decisions, the SFP would have pursued that. In traditional psychotherapy approaches, the direction of the session would likely have immediately shifted to exploring the client's feelings about the break-up of her relationship.

[4]Notice how the SF Practitioner continues to ask questions in order to clarify the goal.

[5]It is not unusual for clients' thoughts and ideas to meander during the goal development process at the beginning of the session and clients' goals sometimes shift during the session. The SF practitioner must continue to ask questions until both the client and SFP have agreed on a clear goal for the session.

Erin: Exactly.

SF Practitioner: Let's suppose you accomplish that goal, what will that look like?

Erin: Well, first of all, I won't be spending my time worrying about how I will be paying the rent on my apartment and spending my weekends all alone crying over a guy who suddenly left me after a five year relationship.

SF Practitioner: What will you be doing instead? **(SF Instead Question)**.

Erin: I know I would be feeling better. I'd be having a happier, better life — how I want to feel, but it is kind of hard to define what it looks like in real life. Maybe I am just spinning dreams, maybe it's all just hopeless. (She looks downcast).

SF Practitioner: What has it looked like at other times in your life when you have felt happier? **(SF Exception Question)**.

Erin: I was almost always in a good mood. People would comment on the fact that I was always smiling.

SF Practitioner: So you would be smiling and in a good mood. What are some of the things that you like to do when you are in a good mood? **(SF Exception Question)**.

Erin: I like to spend time out doors. I like to go on walks. I like to go hiking and skiing and camping. That is why I wanted to move here. I like living in places where I can have an outdoor lifestyle.

SF Practitioner: You would be enjoying living in a place like this where you could have an outdoor lifestyle. What else do you do when you are feeling happier?

Erin: I spend time with friends. I used to spend time with my boyfriend. I really thought we were happy together, but apparently he wasn't or he wouldn't have left.

SF Practitioner: There is a question that helps clarify things in situations like this, but it requires that you use your imagination and it takes some effort to answer. Would you be willing to give it a try?

Erin: Okay.

SF Practitioner: Let's suppose that tonight you go back to your apartment and you do whatever would be normal for you on this kind of evening. It gradually gets later and you eventually get tired. Eventually you go to bed and you fall into a nice deep sleep. Sometime while you are sleeping something very unusual happens. It is a sort of miracle in which you are suddenly transported to the point at which you have become in every possible way that kind of person who is absolutely able to leave by the front door. But of course, since this miracle happened while you were sleeping, when you wake up you don't realise that anything is different until you start moving on with your day. What do you suppose will be the first thing you notice after you wake up that will tell you that something major has changed, that you have now become this 'Front Door' kind of person? **(SF Miracle Question)**.

Erin: I don't know ...

SF Practitioner: Take as much time as you need ... .

Erin: (After several seconds of silence) I guess the first thing that I would notice is that I would have some really good food in the refrigerator and that I would be making myself a nice breakfast.

SF Practitioner: What would you find yourself eating for breakfast on this miracle day?

Erin: I would eat some beautiful fresh fruit, probably some strawberries. Since it is a miracle, they would be in season and already cleaned, right? (SFP nods). And I would have some scrambled eggs and toast, and a good cup of coffee with real cream in it.

SF Practitioner: What happens next?

Erin: I would get dressed and ready for work.

SF Practitioner: What would that look like?

Erin: People in my profession dress really casually, so I would probably have taken a shower and be dressed in a nice hoodie and some jeans. And my hair would have been recently styled, so it would look nice.

SF Practitioner: What happens next on this day after the miracle?

Erin: I would go into work. Ideally I would walk to work and the weather would be nice.

SF Practitioner: What happens next?

Erin: I would go into the office, say hello to my co-workers, fix a cup of coffee for myself, and start working. I would like doing my work.

SF Practitioner: What happens next?

Erin: I would eat a quick lunch, but it would be a healthy one. And then I would get back to work on whatever project I was doing, and at the end of the day I would leave with a good feeling.

SF Practitioner: What sorts of thing would you be doing or saying while you are having this good feeling at the end of the day?[6]

Erin: I would probably be smiling at people who happened to cross my path while I walked home. I might make a comment about the weather.

SF Practitioner: What happens next on this miracle day?

Erin: I would walk into my apartment and things would look nice. It would be my happy place. I wouldn't see dirty dishes in the sink and empty spaces on the wall where my former boyfriend's art used to hang.

SF Practitioner: What does your happy place look like—what would you see instead when you walk into your apartment on the day after the miracle?

Erin: The walls would be painted a fresh new color that I really liked, probably a very soft grey or a very gentle shade of yellow. Everything would be

---

[6]Asking what she would be doing or saying while experiencing good feelings elicits a behavioral description that subsequently makes it easier for the client to later replicate.

put away and orderly. Maybe a cleaning person would have been there that day. I would have a cozy new couch with some fun pillows on it.

SF Practitioner: What happens next after this miracle?

Erin: It's a miracle, right? So I would have tickets for the night to see my favorite band? I would be meeting friends for a quick dinner before the concert. It would be something that I had been looking forward to. (She is smiling).

SF Practitioner: What happens after the concert?

Erin: I come home and I am not alone. I have a new friend and we spend some time playing some new video games before he eventually goes home. It is a Friday night so I don't have to worry about getting up in the morning.

SF Practitioner: What happens next?

Erin: I go to sleep looking forward to the weekend.

SF Practitioner: This sounds nice.

Erin: It would be great ... I wish that was really the way my life was right now.

SF Practitioner: Is it okay if I draw a little scale to help us figure out how to make this happen?[7]

Erin: Okay.

SF Practitioner: Imagine a 0–10 scale where the 10 represents that you are happily living exactly the way you described in the miracle you described and 0 signifies the exact opposite. (She takes out a piece of paper and draws a horizontal line with 0 the far left and 10 on the far right, writes The Miracle above the 10 and The Opposite above the 0, gives the piece of paper to Erin along with a pencil). *I would like you to make a mark on the scale to represent where you are now.* **(SF Scaling Question).**

0————————————————————————————————10

Erin: (She accepts the paper and pencil, hesitates a moment, and then marks the paper slightly to the right of the 2).

SF Practitioner: What number does that signify for you? **(SF Scaling Question).**

Erin: 2 or 3. I guess it is a 2.

SF Practitioner: What makes it a 2.5 and not lower? **(SF Scaling Question).**

Erin: I have a job interview on Friday, and my name is on the apartment lease.

SF Practitioner: Those parts of the Miracle are clearly already in place. Is there anything else that the 2.5 represents? **(SF Scaling Question).**

---

[7]People are usually very willing to answer SF Scaling Questions if their purpose has first been explained.

Erin: It represents the fact that I already have jobs skills, a university degree in IT, and good references. Actually when I say this, it seems to me that the number should be more like a 3.[8]

SF Practitioner: Taking your job skills, degree, already existing work skills, and good references into account raises the number to a 3? **(SF Scaling Question)**.

Erin: Yes.

SF Practitioner: (She hands the paper and pencil back to Erin).

Erin: (She crosses out the previous mark on the scale and draws a new one approximately in the position of 3).

SF Practitioner: I realise that the 10 represents the ideal, but is there any number somewhere between the 3 and the 10 that would somehow be although not perfect more or less good enough? **(SF Scaling Question)**.[9]

Erin: Actually, I think that an 8 would be good enough.

SF Practitioner: Let's suppose you are at an 8. What will be happening?

Erin: At an 8, I would have a new job, my apartment would be painted, and everything would be clean and uncluttered. And I would have started eating healthy again. **(SF Scaling Question)**.

SF Practitioner: That sounds enjoyable.

Erin: It would be. (She is smiling.).

SF Practitioner: I think you have done a very good job of describing this. **(SF Direct Compliment)**.

Erin: Thanks.

SF Practitioner: Let's suppose that you suddenly found yourself one point higher on the scale, what would be different?[10]

Erin: I would have picked out some colors, and purchased some paint, paint brushes, paint rollers, and a drop cloth in order to start painting the kitchen. Actually, I think I have already decided on the color

SF Practitioner: You have already picked out the color?! (Her tone is very appreciative). **(SF Indirect Compliment)**.

Erin: I know how I want it to look.

SF Practitioner: Before we end today, I want to take a moment to tell you how impressed I am with how clear you are about the kind of future you want, what you described as having the ability to leave by the Front Door if you want to do so. **(SF Direct Compliment)**. How did you learn to become so skilled at creatively figuring things out like this? **(SF Indirect Compliment)**.

---

[8]It is not unusual for a clients' scaling numbers to go up a little bit during an SFT session.

[9]The purpose of this question is to reduce the distance between the client's current position and the goal, thereby making it less intimidating to the client.

[10]This is another version of the SF Scaling question, *What would it take to move up a point? Some people find it easier to answer scaling questions in which they imagine suddenly being a point higher and others* prefer the other version.

Erin: I think it is perhaps because I am trained as an IT Designer. We have to be creative.

SF Practitioner: That it very interesting. — I will be very interested to hear what you decided to do next. I would like to invite you to simply notice anything that helps you to move up on your scale between now and next time we meet, assuming you would like to come back again.

Erin: Okay. I will do that. I definitely would like to come back. I will schedule a time with your receptionist on the way out.

SF Practitioner: I am looking forward to hearing what you discover.

SESSION ENDS

SF CASE EXAMPLE: LEAVING BY THE FRONT DOOR SESSION 2

The SF Practitioner and Erin begin by exchange greetings.

Erin: I am happy to say that the weather is much nicer today. I love the springtime sunshine.

SF Practitioner: It really is lovely, isn't it?

Erin: Yes — it really is.

SF Practitioner: I notice that you have a smile on your face today. What's better since last time we met?[11]

Erin: I am a 6 on my scale.

SF Practitioner: Wow—how did you do that? **(SF Indirect Compliment).**

Erin: I filed two more job application since we met and I am still in the running for the position I told you about last time. I am feeling pretty confident that I am going to be offered one of them ... And some other things have gotten better as well.

SF Practitioner: That is wonderful! **(SF Direct Compliment).** *What else has gotten better?*

Erin: I not only bought the paint, but I also finished painting my kitchen. I painted it yellow! And I really like the way it looks.

SF Practitioner: That's great! It sounds beautiful. **(SF Direct Compliment).** *Not that there necessarily should be, but is there anything else that has gotten better?*

Erin: (She pauses for a moment. She is clearly thinking). I have started eating a little bit healthier. Not to the degree that I want to, but definitely better than I was doing before.

---

[11]Whenever possible to do so respectfully, SF practitioners try to begin follow-up sessions by talking about anything that has gotten better. This sets a positive atmosphere conducive to solution building.

SF Practitioner: How did you manage to do that? **(SF Indirect Compliment).**

Erin: I kept intending to do a major shopping trip, but I never found time for that. But I did manage to pick up some fresh fruit and yogurt at the local convenience store.

SF Practitioner: I think that I recall you saying last time that you wanted to start eating more fresh fruits.

Erin: Yes, I am not there yet, but I am now at least moving in that direction.

SF Practitioner: The job applications, the new paint in the kitchen, feeling more confident about getting a job, picking up fresh fruit — are all these things part of the 6 on your scale?

Erin: Definitely.

SF Practitioner: This is already a lot, but nevertheless is there anything else that I should perhaps ask about in terms of your 6? **(SF Scaling Question).**

Erin: No, I think that is pretty much all.

SF Practitioner: I recall your saying last time that an 8 on the scale would be your good enough number. How confident are you feeling about continuing to move up on your scale?

Eric: In terms of the scale we talked about last week, which I actually think of as the Able to Leave by the Front Door scale, I would say that I am very confident that I can get to an 8. This might sound funny, but I am a 10 on a 0–10 confidence scale about getting to an 8 on the Leave by Front Door scale.

SF Practitioner: It DOES sound a little bit funny, but in fact I think I understand what you are saying ... I am so impressed with what you have accomplished since last time we met! **(SF Direct Compliment).** *I wondering if you think it would be helpful to talk further about your Able to Leave by the Front Door Scale, or if there is something else that we should discuss today. What do you think would be most helpful?*[12]

Erica: Actually I wanted to talk to you about a situation that has come up with my ex-boyfriend. He says that he wants to come over and spend some time with me or maybe have us meet to lunch. He says that he wants to be friends. I am not sure that I feel comfortable doing that. The way he chose to leave was very painful. What do you think?

SF Practitioner: I think that this is your decision to make and that you have just now done a very good job of summing up the situation and expressing

---

[12]This question clearly demonstrates the inherently collaborative nature of the SFT approach. In contrast to traditional psychotherapy models that automatically assume that the expert rather than the client is best equipped to know what is needed, SF practitioners ask their clients what they think will be most helpful.

how you feel. I wonder if it would be helpful to answer him in more or less the same words.[13]

Erin: I just want to be sure that I am being fair and reasonable.

SF Practitioner: What would tell you afterwards that you had been fair and reasonable?

Erin: I would feel more at peace if I know I have been fair.

SF Practitioner: Let's imagine a 0–10 scale in which 10 represents you feeling completely at peace l, and 0 signifies whatever the opposite of peace means for you. (Erin nods). Now let's suppose you imagine that you have met your ex-boyfriend for lunch and you have spent some time with him. Where would you rate that experience in terms of feeling at peace?[14]

Erin: I think … . It would be something like a 3. I would be glad that it was over and that I hopefully would not need to do it again. It would mostly be a sense of relief that I had done it this once and that I didn't have to go through it again.

SF Practitioner: Ok. Now let's suppose that you decided not to meet with your boyfriend and you have told him that you are not going to see him for dinner or at meet at the apartment. Where does that scenario put you on the Peacefulness Scale?

Erin: Honestly?

SF Practitioner: Of course.

Erin: I think it is about a 6.

SF Practitioner: Does that number feel ok to the degree it would be good enough or perhaps more accurately allows you feel sufficiently peaceful?

Erin: I don't know … actually, I am afraid it doesn't.

SF Practitioner: What would need to happen or what might you be able to do or say in order for you to afterwards feel more peaceful about either seeing him or choosing to not see him?

Erin: That is a good question but it's a hard question … .[15] *(She pauses, clearly thinking …) I guess I would need to tell him that I am not comfortable seeing him at this point, but that maybe I might feel more comfortable about it at some point in the future after some time had passed and that if that happens I would let him know.*

SF Practitioner: Imagining that you told him exactly what you just said, where would that put you on your Peace scale?

Erin: I feel pretty peaceful. Pretty close to a 10.

---

[13]SF practitioners generally refrain from giving advice or offering interpretation.

[14]Although SF Practitioners sometimes physically draw an SF Scale, they do not always do so. In some cases, they simply invite the client to imagine the scale.

[15]Notice that the SF practitioner does not interrupt the client's train of thought but simply waits for the answer.

SF Practitioner: *Is there anything else that would make the number higher, even closer to a 10?*

Erin: *Having some time pass would be the only thing that could make it higher.*

SF Practitioner: *You sound very clear about what response will result in your feeling most at peace afterwards.*

Erin: *I am.*

SF Practitioner: *You said it was a hard question to answer. But somehow you managed to search deep inside yourself for the answer that would allow you to feel at peace.* **(SF Direct Compliment).** *This clearly was not an easy thing to do. How did you manage to find the strength to do it?* **(SF Indirect Compliment).**

Erin: *While I was trying to figure out my answer, I remember thinking that even though he wasn't true to me, I can be true to myself.*

SF Practitioner: *And remembering that was helpful.*

Erin: *It was. But now I have to actually say this to him.*

SF Practitioner: *Imagining a 0–10 scale where 10 means you are completely confident about being able to say these words to your boyfriend and 0 means not at all confident, where would you rate yourself?*

Erin: *(She laughs nervously). I guess I would rate myself at about a 6 or a 7.*

SF Practitioner: *Is that a good enough number or does it need to be higher.*

Erin: *I feel pretty anxious, a little scared that he might suddenly get really angry about me not agreeing to see him at this time — I think I need the number to be higher.*

SF Practitioner: *What would you like to feel instead of anxious?*

Erin: *I would like to feel peaceful and relaxed.*

SF Practitioner: *What are some of the times that you feel peaceful and relaxed?*

Erin: *I feel relaxed when I am taking a walk at the end of the workday. I often talk on the phone to a friend when I am doing that.*

SF Practitioner: *Let's imagine that you are taking a walk at the end of the workday and you are on the phone when you decide to talk to him. What number does that put it on your confidence scale?*

Erin: *Being outside and moving always makes me feel more peaceful and relaxed —— so I think that would Bring my number up to a 8 or a 9. Actually I think it would help if I just told him over the phone. I was thinking that I needed to respond to him in person, but actually there is no reason I couldn't just call him or text him.*

SF Practitioner: *Which of these would allow you to feel most peaceful and relaxed at the time and afterwards?*

Erin: *I think just telling him on the phone. Actually I don't think I want to be walking in the park while I am talking to him on the phone because afterwards I don't want to associate my favorite park with an unpleasant conversation.*

SF Practitioner: What number do you find yourself on your scale when you imagine just telling him on the phone?

Erin: Actually, pretty close to a 10 in terms of confidence if I imagine just doing it and getting it over with; if he does't answer I can just leave him a message. It now feels like what I need to do.

SF Practitioner: And how about your feeling of peacefulness?

Erin: I will feel at peace. Maybe not a 10 but definitely good enough. And I will go on with the rest of my life with a happier heart.

SF Practitioner: You will feel at peace (Erin nods). And you will have a happier heart. What will that look like?

Erin: I will have a job and go to work and I will start to be friendlier with people again, striking up conversations, going to social events, concerts, art exhibits, things I like to do. I'm not in a hurry to get into another serious relationship, but if someone invites me out for coffee and I like them, I will probably go. I wouldn't have said that two weeks ago.

SF Practitioner: You sound clear on what your next steps are going to be.

Erin: I am. I feel relieved.

SF Practitioner: I am very happy to hear this.

Erin: Thanks.

SF Practitioner: Is there anything else that we should talk about or that I should perhaps ask you before we end today?

Erin: No, I think I got what I needed today. Is it okay if I call you in the future for an appointment if I find that I have something that I need to work on or figure out?

SF Practitioner: Absolutely. It has been a pleasure to work with you. **(SF Direct Compliment).**

SESSION ENDS

Follow-Up

The following day, the SF Practitioner received an email from Erin saying that she had called her ex-boyfriend from her car on her cell phone immediately after the appointment and had a short, peaceful conversation in which she told him of her decision. He responded that he respected her decision. They ended by mutually wishing each other happiness in the future. She described that it had been a *bittersweet but ultimately peaceful* interaction and she felt much better and more relaxed.

A few days later, the SF Practitioner received another short email from Erin saying that she had just accepted a job that she really liked and that she was confident that if and when she ever decided to move on to new job in another city, she would definitely be able to leave *by the front door.*

DISCUSSION

This transcript demonstrates the goal-driven core of the SFT approach. Because SFT is characterised by several specific techniques, it might be tempting to conceptualise it as a technique-driven approach. But this would be erroneous. A close reading of the second session transcript demonstrates that SF techniques are invariably selected and utilised in the service of the clients goals. Beginning with the first sessions, the SF Practitioner repeatedly asked various SF Goal Development Questions in order to collaborate on a clear goal, asking for example what the client meant by *being able to leave by the front door*. Following that, the SF Practitioner asked the client the SF Miracle Question to elicit a behavioral description of the solution, and follows up with SF Scaling Questions in order to identify the behavioral steps necessary to achieve it.

In Session 2, the client's goal changes and the SF Practitioner uses additional SF techniques (Exception Questions, What Else, Scaling) to collaborate with the client in creating a sustainable solution. In all instances, SF techniques are utilised in the service of the client's goal, and never vice versa.

In contrast to traditional psychotherapy models that automatically assume that the therapist rather than the client is best equipped to know what is needed, SF Practitioners typically ask their clients what they think will be most helpful. Beginning early in Session 1, the SF Practitioner repeatedly demonstrates this by asking the client *"What will need to happen"* for the session to prove helpful. In Session 2, the SF Practitioner again demonstrates respect for the client's expertise by asking whether it would be more helpful to focus on the previous scale or something else.

As the SFT sessions progress, whenever Erin describes or alludes to a strength or resource **(SF Exception)**, the SF Practitioner encourages her to offer more details, e.g. *Is there anything else,* subsequently offers **SF Direct Compliments** and **SF Indirect Compliments.** Asking about the details of exceptions and offering compliments specific to the client's description of strengths is deliberate on the part of the SF Practitioner. Compliments function to emphasise and punctuate strengths and resources, and asking about details furthers their impact.

In Session 2, when Erin solicits the SF Practitioner's opinion about seeing the ex-boyfriend, the Practitioner responds by validating the clarity of Erin's description and suggesting that she incorporate this into her answer to him. Although they do not hesitate to provide pertinent information when requested by the client or offer it in instances where it is clearly be necessary, SFT Practitioners typically try to refrain from giving advice or offering interpretations. Clients are viewed as the primary experts on their own lives and what they want or need to have happen and the practitioner is considered to be the primary expert on which questions will most effectively elicit the information necessary for fulfilling clients' specific goals.

You may have noticed that the second session begins with the SF Practitioner asking Erica *What's better.* Obviously this is not a question that the SF Practitioner would have begun with if the client was clearly experiencing emotional pain at that moment. However, whenever it possible to do so in a respectful and caring way, SF Practitioners like to begin follow-up sessions by asking about what (if anything) has gotten better, and in instances where nothing has, they ask about whether the client perhaps did something to prevent things from getting worse. This way of beginning a session sets a positive atmosphere conducive to solution building.

When the client pauses before answering a question or comments that *This is a hard question,* SF Practitioners are careful not to interrupt the client's thought process by introducing new information, nor do they repeat the question unless the client asks them to do so. (De Shazer et al., 2021, p. 44). In Session 2, the SF Practitioner waits patiently while the client gradually formulates an answer to *What would need to happen or what might you be able to do or say in order for you to afterwards feel more peaceful about either seeing him or choosing to not see him?*

Session 2 concludes with the client being assured that she will be able to contact the SF Practitioner in the future if needed. This is consistent with the SFT assumption that clients are the primary experts on their own lives and what will make them better and that SF practitioners role is that of collaborator and provider of a complementary but different kind of expertise: Knowing which questions to ask in order to generate solutions.

CHAPTER SUMMARY

A typical SFT session is driven by the client's goals and involves utilising a variety of SF techniques, such as Goal Development Questions, the SF Miracle Question, Exception Questions, Direct and Indirect Complements, and Scaling Questions, for the following purposes:

1. To collaborate with the client in generating a detailed behavioral description of what the client's life will be like when the problem that caused them to seek treatment is gone.
2. To work collaboratively with the client to identify and utilise already existing resources in the client's experiential repertoire needed to develop a sustainable solution.
3. To collaboratively identify the behavioral steps needed in order for the client to achieve and sustain the solution in his or her ongoing everyday life.

EXPERIENTIAL SF EXERCISE: PUTTING A GOAL ON A SCALE

This exercise is designed to provide a direct experience of SF scaling.

Think of some aspect of your every day life that you would like to enhance or improve, e.g. getting regular physical exercise, your relationship with a co-worker, taking time for self-nurturing and relaxation, etc. Imagine a 0–10 scale in which 10 = The Goal Has Already Been Achieved, e.g. you are completely satisfied and 0 = the Opposite. Where would you currently rate yourself on the scale? Let's suppose that you went up a point. What would indicate to you that you had gone up a point on the scale? Describe what being a point closer to your goal it would look like in behavioral terms, e.g. what you will be doing differently. Experiment with implementing this change and notice what happens next.

REFERENCES

Berg, I. K., & Dolan, Y. (2001). *Tales of solutions: A collection of hope inspiring stories*. New York: Norton.

de Shazer, S., Dolan, Y., Korman, H., Trepper, T. S., McCollum, E. E., & Berg, I. K. (2021). *More than miracles: The state of the art of solution-focused brief therapy, 2nd Ed*. New York: Routledge.

SOLUTION-FOCUSED PRACTICES
IN SCHOOL SETTINGS

The SF approach has been applied to classroom management, student advising and counseling, teacher supervision and consultation, parent consultation, and even organising an entire school including teachers, counselors, administration, custodial staff, and food service workers (Franklin et al., 2022). This chapter describes how the SF approach can help grade school teachers manage challenging classrooms; how SFBT can be used by school counselors in elementary, secondary, and college settings; how an entire high school staff used SF practices to encourage and support students who would otherwise be at risk for dropping out; and finally, the chapter provides a case transcript which demonstrates how the SF approach can be used to relieve a very common school-related problem, test anxiety, and enhance a university student's academic performance[1].

CLASSROOM MANAGEMENT

The Working on What Works (WOWW) program for classroom management was the first adaptation of SF practices for school settings. Originally developed by one of SFBT's founders Insoo Kim Berg, and Lee Shilts (Berg & Shilts, 2005), and further developed and studied by Michael Kelly and his team from Loyola University in Chicago (Kelly & Bluestone-Miller, 2009; Kelly et al., 2012), the six to eight-week WOWW program utilises SF principles to

---

[1]While there have been hundreds of scholarly works about the use of SF practices in the schools, this discussion will only be able to provide a sampling of how SF can be effectively used in school settings.

DOI: 10.4324/9781003401230-4

empower teachers and students in regular and special education classes to recognise their own strengths and abilities and progress toward their desired goals. The WOWW program has been shown to improve the management and climate of the classroom (e.g. Brown et al., 2012), increase student on-task behavior (Kelly et al., 2012), decrease disruptive behavior (Fernie & Cubeddu, 2016), and result in fewer days absent from school (Wallace et al., 2020).

How does the WOWW program work? Imagine that a beleaguered teacher is struggling with an unruly class of 4th grade students who have been consistently refusing to remain in their chairs or concentrate on their lessons. With the WOWW program, a coach trained in SF principles and practices sits in on a number of class sessions, observes what is going on, paying particular attention to what the teachers and students are doing that is *working,* and then reports the observations back to the class.

This is what happens when the teacher engages the help of a WOWW coach:

1. The SF coach, after introducing herself and exchanging a few pleasantries,[2] tells the students that she will be visiting their classroom for the next eight weeks to observe the things the students do that are helpful and positive. She subsequently observes the class on several occasions. On each visit she carefully notes what individual students and the class as a whole are doing well and then reports her observations back to the students, for example:

   Today I noticed that several of you did a good job of continuing to focus on your assignment even though there was a lot of noise going on in the hallway outside the classroom. I was very impressed! **(SF Direct Compliment).**

   I also noticed people helping each other, passing out the assignments sheets, taking turns using the art supplies. This shows that you are doing a good job of paying attention to the teacher and also that you were paying attention to each other in a very cooperative, helpful way. **(Direct Compliment).**

---

[2]SF practitioners routinely take a few moments immediately after meeting clients for the first time, and at the beginning of subsequent sessions to "join with the client" by exchanging pleasantries about some neutral every day topic such as the weather, local events, etc. The purpose of this is to help clients relax in a natural way that communicates that the SF practitioners sees them as a fellow human being and not just as a "client," or in this case, a 4th grade student.

I could see that you were very interested in what was going on outside and wanted to get up and go over to the window, but you manage to stay at your desk and concentrate on your work. How did you get yourself to do that? **(SF Indirect Compliment).** The students obviously enjoy being complimented.

2. Following the initial visit, the WOWW coach shows the students a 1–10 point scale in which 10 symbolises the best and 0 the opposite. A gradation of sad faces gradually changing to happy faces is sometimes used for younger children. The coach and teacher then invite the students to describe what the best classroom (symbolised by the 10 or happy face) would look like, what a 5 would like, etc. The students naturally have many specific ideas about this. For example, a 2 might signify that very few students were paying attention, a 1 might signify that several people were wandering around the classroom disturbing others rather than remaining in their seats and working at their desks, 5 might signify that at least half the students were paying careful attention, etc. Following this discussion, the SF coach asks the students to each pick a number on the scale based on how things are going in their classroom today:

What number on the scale would you give your classroom today? (The class is given a score for that day based on an average of the numbers given).

The students are also invited to describe their rationale for the numbers they give:

What do you see happening in class today that makes you give it that number on the scale?

Additionally, the coach might ask:

What would help keep the number at that point? What could have made it go down, and what will make it go up higher?

3. Following each classroom observation session, the WOWW coach also meets privately with the teacher to do similar goal setting and scaling, offer positive feedback on what the teacher is doing that is working, and complimenting.

What would it take for you to rate yourself one point higher on your teaching scale? **(SF Scaling Question).**

Clearly, the way you engaged them today really worked. They were completely absorbed in the science experiment you were demonstrating. **(Direct Compliment).**

DISCUSSION

The compliments that the WOWW coach gave the students at the conclusion of each of the observation sessions typify how SF practitioners join with their clients by focusing on and emphasising their strengths. WOWW coaches join with the classroom teachers in a similar way by respectfully engaging in a collegial manner and making appreciative observations about their teaching skills.

SCHOOL COUNSELING

Solution-Focused Brief Therapy is used by school counselors and psychologists all over the world, with notable programs in Singapore, Korea, England, Sweden, the Netherlands, and in the United States (Franklin et al., 2022). The research done thus far has suggested that SFBT in grade school, high school, and college settings helps reduce the intensity of students' negative feelings, manages conduct problems, and reduces externalising behavioral problems (Beauchemin, 2018; Chen et al., 2018; Kim et al., 2017).

Similar to SFBT in clinical settings, SFBT in school settings consists of the standard SF interventions, all of which are usually incorporated in each session. For example, the Miracle Question or some similarly structured questions are used to help the student set future-oriented goals:

> *Let's suppose that when you woke up tomorrow, sometime during the night when you were sleeping something suddenly happened that would somehow make things go much better for you at school from now on. But since it happened when you were sleeping, you wouldn't know it had happened until you or other people around you started gradually noticing that something had changed and there were some things that were different.*
>
> *What would be the first thing your best friend would notice that was different about you on your Miracle day?*
>
> *What would your teacher notice?*
>
> *What would your parents notice?*
>
> *What would you notice?*
>
> *What else?*

The counselor gently elicits as many positive details from the student as possible regarding what will be happening when things are better, thereby generating a richly evocative detailed personalised description uniquely meaningful to the client. Used skillfully, the **SF Miracle**

Question gives students a vivid, virtual experience of what "better" feels, sounds, and looks like. This provides a virtual mental rehearsal that simultaneously lowers tension, elicits positive emotions, and gradually increases motivation by seeding hope.

SF discussions with student oftentimes focus on discovering whether change, evidenced by new or increased exceptions to the problem, is already occurring, and encouraging the student to continue to do more of the things that are already proving helpful. For example:

> *Are there times when things have been going better for you, maybe in big ways, but also maybe just in some little ways, even just a little bit better? How did you manage to make this happen?* (The counselor gets as many details as possible about any thing positive that the student is doing).

Students who have trouble identifying exceptions oftentimes find it easier to imagine it from another person's point of view:

> *What would your best friend (mother, father, significant other) say is going better for you, even a little bit?*

Students also oftentimes benefit from being asked to scale their goals on a 0–10 point scale (either with numbers or a gradation of sad-happy faces), discussing what they would need to do to move up a point for next session, discussing how they moved up on the scale in subsequent sessions. For example:

> *How would you discover that you had gone up a point on this scale in the next week?*
>
> *What will you be doing that will tell you (the coach, teacher friends, etc.) that you have gone up a point?*
>
> *How will others react?*
>
> *Who will be most likely to notice this first?*

SF school counselors continue to monitor students' progress until the goal has been reached and students feels confident they can continue achieving positive results on their own. Assessing the client's current progress and/or distance from the goal can be accomplished quickly and informally by asking: *Where are you on your scale today?* The simplicity of using the scale to monitor students' current progress and/or challenges makes it easier for busy school counselors to do brief "check-ins" with a large number of students on a day-to-day basis, sometimes even while they are simply passing by in the hall. And because scales utilise numbers rather than verbal descriptions to signify the current distance from the goal, the students' confidentiality and privacy are preserved in the presence of other teachers or students.

As illustrated in several of the previous examples, SFBT school counselors often invite students to expand their solution description to include friends, family, and teachers as exemplified by SF questions like:

> *How would your mother know that you had achieved your miracle?*
>
> *What would be the first thing your best friend would notice when you are a 9 on the scale?*
>
> *How do our suppose your teacher would react if you managed to get through the whole week without being sent to the Principal's office? How surprised do you think she might be?*

School counselors trained in SFT learn to listen carefully for signs and signals of SF exceptions to the students' problems and for solutions that have already begun to occur:

> *You said that even though you don't like school, you go to school sometimes, anyway: What about those times that you go?* **(SF Exception Question).**
>
> *How do you manage to get yourself to do this?* **(SF Coping Question).**

Not surprisingly, students are typically more willing and motivated to engage in identifying and honing skills and abilities than to focus on correcting problems. While focusing on correcting a problem can evoke painful memories of past failures and feelings of personal inadequacy, focusing on skills and abilities can feel more like an adventure or a challenge.

Overall, the SF approach to school counseling assumes that major changes can occur as a result of small shifts in how students talk and think about their lives. Solution-talk is usually far more productive and helpful than problem-talk.

PARENT-TEACHER CONSULTATION

Many teachers have found the SF approach to be a particularly helpful way to approach talking to parents about their child's progress (cf Gillies, 2013). Teachers trained in SF have noted that parent conferences, even with parents of students who are currently struggling in school, are less stressful, more collaborative, and more positive. Similar to the SF applications to education described earlier in this chapter, the particular elements of the SF approach that teachers and school counselors usually find to be most helpful in structuring a parent-teacher meeting include:

- Focusing on the student's strengths and abilities, as opposed to his or her deficits and problems.
- Identifying the student's resources and how the teacher is working to utilise those.
- Having the parents identify changes and exceptions their child has demonstrated during the school year, and encouraging them to do more of what they may be doing that helps.
- Asking the parents the Miracle Question, followed by scaling questions about the student's current distance from the Miracle.
- Complimenting the parents for behaviors that are supportive to their child.

A SOLUTION-FOCUSED ALTERNATIVE SCHOOL

One of the most ambitious and exciting possibilities is to design an entire school to be solution-focused. When this is done, it provides a complete solution-focused educational context which permeates all aspects of the student's and staff's school experience which emphasises hopeful, positive, empowering language; experimenting with new behavioral patterns; and encouraging incremental change. Students are viewed as being experts in identifying their own solutions to problems, and thus student input is valued and sought after by teachers and staff.

The first all-school solution-focused school was at Garza High School in Austin, Texas (Franklin et al., 2012; Franklin et al., 2018). Designated for high-risk high school students (e.g. students who were at high-risk for leaving school before graduation), this alternative school was deliberately redesigned into an SF institution in order to better address a variety of problems including high dropout rates, low rates of college enrollment among its graduates, and poor academic performance of its students.

The school's administration, led by its principal, aligned with solution-focused researchers from the University of Texas and carefully redesigned the school so that its guiding philosophy was solution-focused, and to make all the various aspects of the student experience reflect the solution-focused approach. In order to accomplish this, everyone working at the school was trained in the SF approach, principles, and techniques, including administrators, teachers, support staff, cafeteria, and custodial staff, and of course the students. The main features of the Garza program were:

- Focusing on goals via a future orientation rather than the past. Students were continuously goal setting and evaluating their movement toward those goals.
- Self-paced learning replaced all students moving through the curriculum at the same time.
- Individualisation allowed students not only to self-pace their movement through a course of study but also to choose the order in which they could take classes using a schedule that worked best for them.
- The staff focused on building on students' competencies, by being given the responsibility to control their own learning, and being empowered to take responsibility for their own progress.
- Support and reciprocal respect among teachers, administrators, staff, and students using solution-focused interventions such as focusing on the positive, looking for exceptions to problems, and complimenting were continuously offered.

Among the most striking results were increased student retention, improved test scores, and higher graduation rates. In addition, students from Garza were more likely to earn high school credits and enter college (Franklin et al., 2007). Garza High School was also selected by the US Department of Education as one of the top dropout prevention and academic success programs (Kim et al., 2019).

ACADEMIC PERFORMANCE

The SFT approach has been applied to enhancing academic performance, such as academic attitude, academic behavior, and academic performance (Franklin et al., 2022). For example, after school SFBT tutoring sessions were found to be more effective in improving literacy skills, reading motivation, reading practice, and self-esteem than traditional homework-support methods (Daki & Savage, 2010). Other research has found that applications of SFT can improve overall academic motivation (e.g. Golmohamadi & Kimiyaee, 2014), studying (e.g. Huang et al., 2014), and overall classroom performance (Wallace et al., 2020).

Case Example

The following transcript demonstrates how SF principles can be applied to helping a student with an extremely common academic concern: Debilitating test anxiety.

Angela: *I Need to Pass That Test*

Angela is the recipient of an academic scholarship that pays for her college tuition, textbook expenses, and housing costs on the condition that she maintain an above-average grade point average. A diligent, hardworking student, her grades had always been in the top percentage of her class. She was therefore shocked and frightened when after studying for a test late into the night, she received an unexpectedly low score. Desperate to maintain her grade point average so as to avoid losing her scholarship, Angela immediately scheduled an appointment at the school's Student Counseling Center where she was seen by a solution-focused practitioner.

Solution-Focused Practitioner: (After exchanging informal greetings) *What are your best hopes for how this appointment can be helpful?* **(SF Goal Development Question).**

Angela: I just got a really low grade on an exam that I had studied hard for. I was feeling nervous before the exam because I hadn't gotten around to studying for it until the night before, but I definitely didn't expect to do so poorly. I was just a little bit nervous at first, but then it started getting worse and worse once I started taking the test. I got so panicked that I couldn't even remember some of the things I had studied just the night before and that I know could have easily remembered earlier that morning. I just kept panicking and panicking more. My heart was pounding and I could barely breathe. Somehow I got through it, but I had a very uncomfortable feeling afterwards, and it turned out that I got a below average grade. If I don't get a really good grade on the next test, I might be at risk for losing my scholarship. I am scared!

Solution-Focused Practitioner: Of course. This must be really difficult for you. Is your main goal to get a good grade on the next test? **(SF Goal Development Question).**

Angela: Yes, but it is more than that. I don't want to panic like that again. I got so anxious while I was taking the test that I couldn't concentrate; I was so nervous that I couldn't remember many of the things that I knew, even some of the material I had just studied the night before.

Solution-Focused Practitioner: Next time you want to be able to stay calm enough to remember the material you studied? **(SF Goal Development Question).**

Angela: Yes! I don't want to feel so anxious!

Solution-Focused Practitioner: You want to pass the next test with a good grade and you don't want to feel anxious beforehand?

Angela: Exactly.

Solution-Focused Practitioner: What do you want to be feeling instead of anxiety? **(SF Instead Question).**

Angela: I want to feel calm. Or at least as calm and centered as I always did before this happened, But right now I have another test coming up at the end of the week and I am so nervous about it that I am afraid I am going to do badly again even if I study really hard. I don't know what to do.

Solution-Focused Practitioner: This is really hard for you right now and I can see why you definitely want to get things back on track as soon as possible.

Angela: Yes, that's exactly what I want. But the problem is that right now even thinking about taking the next test makes me start feeling anxious.

Solution-Focused Practitioner: Of course. And you want to get back to that more calm feeling of being centered and doing well on your tests that is usually normal for you? **(SF Goal Development Question).**

Angela: Exactly. But I have no idea how to do it.

SF Practitioner: There is this kind of strange question that can be especially useful in figuring out what will be most helpful in situations like this.[3] Is it okay if I ask you a strange question that oftentimes helps in situations like this?

Angela: Okay.

Solution-Focused Practitioner: Let's suppose that tonight you go home and it eventually it gets later. You start to get tired and after doing the things that you normally would do, you eventually go to bed and you fall asleep. And sometime during the night a sort of miracle happens. The miracle is that now you are at a 10 on the scale we just talked about. Everything has returned to normal, you know just what to do in order to get good scores on your exams, and your confidence is back. But of course you wouldn't know this when you first wake up because this miracle happened during the night when you were sleeping. What do you suppose would be the first thing that you or maybe someone else might notice that would cause you to start realising that the problem was gone and you were back to normal **(SF Miracle Question).**

Angela: I don't know ... .[4] I guess the first thing I would notice at is that I wouldn't have this feeling of dread when I woke up.

SF Practitioner: What would you be feeling instead? **(Instead Question).**

Angela: I would be thinking about what I needed to do that day. Usually I get up pretty early so I can have some coffee before class, or if its a weekend, so I can get all my studying out of the way by early afternoon.

SF Practitioner: So what happens next? **(SF Detail Question).**

---

[3]This is a small but important detail: Note that the SF practitioner introduces the question by first clarifying that it is likely to be helpful and then asking permission before proceeding.

[4]Perhaps because formulating an answer to the SF Miracle Question entails some time, people typically preface their answers with *I don't know* before eventually answering. SF practitioners learn to give their clients as much time as they need by either remaining silent or offering gentle encouragement, e.g. take as much time as you need...

Angela: I am going to assume that it is a weekend because today is Friday. After poured my first cup of coffee, I would sit down and start studying. I would do that until about 11:30, then I would go for a quick three mile run, come home, take a shower, get something to eat and then study for another hour or so depending on what I needed to get done. That night I would probably spend time with my boyfriend.

SF Practitioner: What would your boyfriend perhaps notice that was different about you that might give him the idea that something was different after this Miracle had happened, that things were somehow back to normal in terms of your usual study habits that work for you and your level of confidence? **(SF Detail Question).**

Angela: He might notice that I seemed more relaxed. I suppose that the big thing he would notice is that I wouldn't stay at his place on Sunday night even though he always wants me to do that. I would come home Sunday afternoon, get my things together for the coming week, do a little studying, and get a good night sleep.

SF Practitioner: Let's suppose you do that, how would he likely react? **(SF Detail Question).**

Angela: He probably won't like it. He's been sort of pressuring me to spend more and more time with him. He is not in school right now, so I think he forgets how important it is to study, at least for people like me whose scholarships depend on maintaining a good grade point average.

SF Practitioner: So let's suppose he tries to get you to stay. Since this Miracle has now happened you now know exactly what to do. How do you react? **(SF Detail Question).**

Angela: I would be nice about it, but I would tell him very firmly, 'No, I need to go home,' and if he argued, I would just say, 'Sorry, but I am going home now.'

SF Practitioner: So you would go home. What else will people notice you doing after this Miracle? **(SF Detail Question).**

Angela: My roommate will notice that I am home more during school nights. And she'll see a smile on my face.

SF Practitioner: You'll be home more and you'll be smiling more. What else might people notice after this Miracle? **(SF Detail Question).**

Angela: I don't know if any of my classmates or teachers will necessarily notice, but I will be more or less back to my old self.

SF Practitioner: What does this 'back to your old self' look like?[5] **(SF Detail Question).**

Angela: I wouldn't be depressed. I would have my usual energy. I would probably be singing in the shower, joking around with my roommate and

---

[5]SF practitioners oftentimes ask what something will "look like" as a way to generate behavioral descriptions. Behavioral descriptions are important because behaviors are typically easier for people to replicate than emotions.

our friends. I would be getting my studying done and my papers finished without staying up all night in order to get them in on time.

SF Practitioner: What would your teachers notice? **(SF Detail Question).**

Angela: I am not sure how much they notice their students on a day-to-day basis, but I guess my physics professor would perhaps notice that I got a good grade on my next exam.

SF Practitioner: Let's suppose you get a good grade on your physics exam. How will you react to that? **(SF Detail Question).**

Angela: I will feel good, like things are back to normal for me.

SF Practitioner: Would that mean that you accomplished your goal? **(SF Goal Development Question).**

Angela: Yes. It would mean that things are back to normal the way I want them to be.

SF Practitioner: Just to make sure that we[6] do not overlook anything, was there anything else that will be different after the Miracle?[7] **(SF Detail Question).**

Angela: The only thing I can think of is I guess I would be more assertive with my boyfriend and my friends too when they ask me to go out to clubs with them on school nights. I would be better at making sure that I give myself enough time to study.

SF Practitioner: What would that be like for you?[8] **(SF Detail Question).**

Angela: He probably won't like it so much at first, but I will be feeling a lot calmer and less pressured for time. But he is a good guy and I think he would eventually respect that I need to do what's necessary to keep my scholarship.

SF Practitioner: And it sounds like keeping your scholarship is a significant part of your goal.

Angela: Yes. It is a huge part.

SF Practitioner: Is there anything else that you can think of that would be different on the day after the Miracle? **(SF Detail Question).**

Angela: No, I think that is pretty much it. (She is visibly calmer after describing the Miracle).[9]

---

[6]Notice how the SF practitioner uses the word *we*. This is a small but important detail because it respectfully communicates that developing the solution is a collaborative process between Angela and the practitioner.

[7]Whenever in doubt, SF practitioners ask *is anything else in* order to ensure that some important detail of the solution is not inadvertently overlooked.

[8]Asking what this will be like for Angela is a way to assess whether this part of the solution is going to be viable for her given the reality of her current relationship.

[9]Answering the SF Miracle question typically generates positive emotions while simultaneously generating a behavioral description of various essential components of a practical solution.

Solution-Focused Practitioner: Now that you have described your miracle, we need to figure out how you can start moving in that direction. The best way that I know to do that is to diagram it on a scale. Is it okay if I draw a scale to help us figure this out?[10]

Angela: Okay.

SF Practitioner: (She draws a horizontal line on a sheet of paper with a 0 at the left end of the line and a 10 at the right end.

0————————————————————————————————10

Let's suppose that there is a 0–10 scale on which 10 represents the day after the Miracle and 0 represents just the Opposite[11] *Where would you put yourself now?* **(Scaling Question).**

Angela: Not very good. Maybe a 3.

Solution-Focused Practitioner: (She makes a short vertical mark just slightly over 1/3 of the way across the scale and draws a 3 over it.)

0———————————/————————————————————————10

Does that | mark look like it is in in the correct position to represent a 3?

Angela: Yes. That looks like where a 3 should be.[12]

Solution-Focused Practitioner: What contributes to making it a 3 as opposed to a lower number?[13] **(SF Scaling Question).**

Angela: Even though I am really scared right now and worried about panicking again, I know that I pretty consistently done well on exams in the past.

Solution-Focused Practitioner: Your history of doing well contributes to the 3. You are accustomed to doing well on your tests.

---

[10]Notice how the SF practitioner explains the purpose of the scaling question and requests permission before asking it. This reflects the overall transparency of the SF approach. And answering scaling questions typically has a calming effect which helps people think more clearly.

[11]By designating "0" to represent just the opposite" of complete confidence, the SF practitioner manages to keep the primary focus on what Angela wants (confidence) instead of focusing further on what she does not want (feelings of panic).

[12]Alternatively, the SF practitioner might have handed Angela the piece of paper with the scale on it and a pencil and asked her to mark the spot that reflected a 3, or just verbally described the scale. However, drawing a physical scale can often prove helpful in clarifying the concept for people new to SF scaling questions.

[13]This question is used to look for details of possible exceptions that may prove useful in developing a solution.

Angela: Yes. I am.

Solution-Focused Practitioner: What else contributes to it being a 3 and not lower[14]? **(SF Detail question)**.[15]

Angela: I know how to study. I normally have good study skills.

Solution-Focused Practitioner: You already have good study skills. So those parts of the Miracle are already in place? **(SF Detail Question)**.

Angela: (She nods). Those things are already in place, but I want to get my confidence back.

Solution-Focused Practitioner: Of course. Assuming that 10 meant completely confident and 0 meant just the opposite,[16] where would you put your confidence on your scale at the moment?[17] **(SF Scaling Question)**.

Angela: I think I would have said a 3 a moment ago, but I think it has gone up a little bit since we talked about my study skills. I think it is now something like a 3 1/2 or a 4.

Solution-Focused Practitioner: And while I imagine that you probably want it to be at a 10, do you think there is there any number between that 3 1/2 or 4 and the 10 that you think might possibly be, although not perfect, perhaps more or less good enough?[18] **(SF Detail Question)**.

Angela: I think an 8 1/2 or a 9 would be good enough. I would still be a little bit worried, but it would be manageable.

SF Practitioner: An 8 1/2 or a 9 would be good enough. And you are currently at a 3(Angela nods). What would need to happen in the next 24 hours in order for you to either maintain that 3 or move up even a little bit? **(SF Scaling Question)**.

---

[14]"And not lower" ensures that the client focuses on the resources inherent in the 3. Words that place the focus on existing resources are more useful for solution development than words that are oriented toward negativity, e.g., "only a 3."

[15]Asking questions about the details of a resource tends to further strengthen it. Since the 3 reflects some of Angela's confidence and knowledge about what she needs to do, it constitutes an exception that can be incorporated into the solution.

[16]Designating 0 as the "opposite" of the desired goal rather than defining it as "failing the test" allows Angela to identify her distance from the goal without unnecessarily creating a mental image of failing a future test. This avoids unnecessarily triggering further feelings of anxiety and keeps the focus on Angela's aspiration rather than on her fears.

[17]A particular advantage of using an SF scale is that the same number can be used to simultaneously represent several things for the client.

[18]SF practitioners sometimes ask their clients to imagine what would be *good enough* as a way to shorten the distance between the goal and the client's current position, thereby rendering it more approachable and oftentimes more realistically achievable.

Angela: (She pauses for several seconds before answering). *My Grandma always told me that I could do whatever I set my mind to. She's dead now, but I have never forgotten what she said to me.*

SF Practitioner: It sounds like what she said to you was very important, and it made a difference for you? **(SF Detail Question).**[19]

Angela: It really did. My grandma always believed in me even at times when I wasn't sure whether I believed in myself.

SF Practitioner: What happens when you remember her saying that you can do whatever you set your mind to? **(SF Detail Question).**[20]

Angela: I miss her of course. But I also believe in myself more when I imagine her saying that.

SF Practitioner: What do you think she saw in you that told her that you could do whatever you set your mind to?

Angela: She was a very accomplished person. She immigrated to the United States when she was 17. She didn't even have a high school education, but she managed to learn English and then to take classes at night in order to get her high school diploma. She cleaned houses all day and then went to school at night. By the time I knew her, she was Head of Housekeeping at a large hotel. Everyone who worked there knew her and respected her. She always said that I was cut out of the same cloth as she was and that I wasn't afraid of hard work.

SF Practitioner: That sounds like a very significant compliment especially coming from someone like her.

Angela: It was.

SF Practitioner: Let's suppose that focus on your grandmother's words, 'You can do anything you put your mind to' and that you are 'cut out of the same cloth' as her. How does remembering those words effect where you are on your confidence scale? **(SF Scaling Question).**

Angela: I start feeling more confident. Maybe more like a 5.

SF Practitioner: A 5! Remembering that clearly makes a difference. How wonderful that you had a grandmother like that and also that you have the good sense to pay attention to what she said! **(SF Direct Compliment)**. *How did you know to do that?* **(Indirect compliment)**. *What effect do you think it would have if you keep focusing on what she said and keep reminding yourself of her words in the coming days?* **(SF Detail Question).**

Angela: I know it will help.

---

[19]This could arguably also be considered an **SF Exception Question** because this memory is clearly a resource for Angela that has the potential to raise her confidence level and help her move in the direction of her goal.

[20]Notice how this question invites the client to further connect to her own strengths, e.g. believing in herself more.

SF Practitioner: What else could you do in the next 24 hours to either maintain where you are with your confidence or to perhaps find yourself[21] going forward even a little? **(SF Scaling Question).**

Angela: Studying. And also having a talk with my boyfriend. I am not blaming him for my bad grade and how anxious I got, but I need to get back on track with my normal study routine. I can't keep going out every night.

SF Practitioner: Let's suppose you do those things: You talk to him and you get back on track with your normal study routine. Where will that put you on the scale? **(SF Scaling Question).**

Angela: It will put me at about a 6 1/2 or a 7.

SF Practitioner: A 6 1/2 or a 7. That brings you significantly closer to your goal.

Angela: Yes, it does.

SF Practitioner: How confident are you that you can talk to him and that you can get back to your normal study routine?[22] **(SF Detail Question).**

Angela: I am quite confident about those two things. Not quite as confident about my tests.

SF Practitioner: What do you think will likely be most helpful in becoming more confident about your tests?

Angela: I need to get good grades in my next two or three tests, especially my next physics test.

SF Practitioner: Where will that put you on the scale?

Angela: Definitely an 8 1/2, but it will get higher after a while if I keep getting good test scores.

SF Practitioner: I think you have done a really good job of figuring this out **(Direct compliment),** *and that you know what you need to do — is that right?* **(Indirect compliment).** *(Angela nods). And I am very impressed with how clear you are about your goals.* **(Direct compliment).** *Is there anything else that I perhaps should have asked or that you think might be important to tell me?* **(SF Safety Net Question).**

Angela: No, I think that covers it.

---

[21] "Finding yourself going forward" is an example of how SF practitioners are deliberatively attentive to language; choosing whenever possible words that characterise the process of moving in the direction of the goal feels less intimidating and more "user friendly."

[22] This question functions to ensure that this behavioral part of the client's solution is realistically something that she feels able to do. If the client does not feel sufficiently confident, the SF practitioner will need to collaboratively address this with the client by finding additional resources to increase her confidence level.

SF Practitioner: In that case I would like to invite you, between now and next time we meet, to pay attention to anything that you do or that anyone else does that contributes to you moving up on your scale.[23]
Angela: Ok.

SUMMARY OF SUBSEQUENT SESSIONS

Angela was seen for two subsequent sessions. The following week Angela reported that:

I passed this week's physics quiz with a good grade. I am currently between a 6 1/2 or a 7 on my Confidence Scale. I am not yet where I want to be with this but I know that I am moving in the right direction and it is ok if it takes some time. I had a fight with my boyfriend but we eventually got past it and we are still together. I am working on balancing my own needs and responsibilities with our relationship; it is not always easy, but I feel like I am moving in the right direction. It helps to remember what my grandmother said.

I ask myself the scaling question every day, and I remind myself of my dream of becoming a licensed veterinarian. I have a poster of a dog on my wall that says, 'Follow your dreams.'

Angela subsequently described that SF Self-Scaling had helped her to stay focused on her own goals, and that she was honoring what she needed to do to be true to herself and her dreams despite the wide variety of entertaining diversions constantly available in the University town where she lived.

A few years later, the SF Practitioner received a card from Angela announcing that she had succeeded with her goal of completing veterinary school and becoming a licensed veterinarian. (Note: Although "Angela" is based on a real-life client, all identifying information has been altered).

DISCUSSION

Beginning and throughout this session, the SF Practitioner made it clear that that helping Angela regain her confidence about test taking was an eminently collaborative process. This was accomplished primarily by

---

[23]Although SF practitioners do not often give specific homework assignments, they oftentimes extend invitations to their clients to observe *(pay attention to)* what works in helping them move in the direction of their goals or experiment their clients with something that has previously worked or looks like it will likely work.

asking questions, but also with the manner that questions were introduced and asked. For example, beginning with the Miracle Question, the SF Practitioner oftentimes explained the purpose of the various questions before introducing them and then asked the client's permission. While this eminently respectful stance typifies the way SF Practitioners work with all their clients, it can have an important reassuring effect for clients like Angela who may be currently struggling with fear about the future and/or performance anxiety.

Rather than asking what would it would "take" in order for Angela to move up on her scale in the direction of her goal, the SF Practitioner asked her to describe w*hat else could you do in the next 24 hours to either maintain where you are with your confidence or to perhaps find yourself* [24] *going forward even a little?* Carefully attentive to language, SF Practitioners deliberately try to choose words that make the process of moving in the direction of the goal feel less intimidating and more "user friendly" for the client. *Finding yourself* going forward, for example, arguably requires less imagined effort than *moving yourself* forward.

The user friendly nature of the SF approach was further exemplified in this session by frequent use of **SF Direct** and **Indirect Compliments**. This session perhaps best exemplifies how SF questions can be used to gently invite hope and generate positive emotions by exploring the specifics of clients' resources and strengths.

Exploring and emphasising the clients' strengths and resources is accomplished in this session not only through SF compliments but also more subtly with the SF Practitioners careful use of language. For example, asking the client what make the number a 3 on the scale and "and not lower" implicitly suggests the inherent value of the resources represented by that number and counteracts any potential negative feelings about it being "only a 3." And since the "3" also reflects Angela's current level of awareness and personal expertise about what she needs to do next in order to move forward on the scale, it constitutes an exception that can be subsequently incorporated into the solution. One of the advantages of

---

[24]"Finding yourself going forward" is an example of how SF practitioners are deliberatively attentive to language, choosing whenever possible, words that characterise the process of moving in the direction of the goal, which feels less intimidating and more "user friendly."

SF scales is that the numbers can simultaneously reflect several different dimensions of the client's current state and the state to which they aspire.

As Angela's movement on the SF Confidence Scale progressed, the SF Practitioner further contributed to making the process "user friendly" by asking if there was a number lower than 10 that although not perfect, would ultimately be "good enough." Despite the inarguable appeal of the "ideal" version, people are usually ultimately relieved and happy to embrace a number on the scale that they would ultimately consider to be "good enough." Assigning the "good enough" number makes the goal less daunting while still retaining the possibility of eventually achieving the ideal version of the goal.

The collaborative nature of the SF approach is further reflected by the coach inviting Angela to *pay attention to anything that you do or that anyone else does that contributes to you moving up on your scale*. This invitation functioned as both an acknowledgment of Angela's expertise and an invitation to utilise SF Scaling as a practical self-help tool that she could potentially continue to use on her own even after the sessions with the SF Practitioner ended. And by the end of the SF counseling process, Angela had begun doing exactly that. Clients continuing to utilise SF Scaling as a self-help tool after therapy ends is a phenomenon frequently described by SF Practitioners.

CHAPTER SUMMARY

The SFT approach has been successfully utilised in elementary schools, middle school, high school, and university settings all over the world for a variety of purposes including classroom management, student retention, teacher parent conferences, alleviating test anxiety, and enhancing academic performance. SFT is used by school counselors, social workers, and psychologists all over the world. Research suggests that SFT helps reduce the intensity of students' negative feelings, manages conduct problems, and reduces externalising behavioral problems in grade school and high school settings.

This chapter described the SF WOWW approach to elementary school classroom management, a high school in which the entire staff was trained in the SF approach, applications of the SF approach to enhance Parent/Teacher communication and enhance academic performance, and an annotated transcription of an SFT counseling session at a university counseling center.

The six- to eight-week WOWW program (Working on What Works) approach to classroom management utilises SF principles to empower teachers and students in regular and special education classes to recognise their own strengths and abilities and progress toward their desired goals. A WOWW coach joins a classroom to serve as a facilitator to help the teacher and students achieve their goals. Skilled WOWW coaches manage to incorporate all of the basic SFBT principles in their sessions.

SF Compliments, SF Goal Development Questions, and SF Scaling Questions are readily applicable to student counseling, teacher supervision and parent-teacher conferences. A Texas high school, for example, trained their entire staff, including administrators, teachers, students, and even support staff, in solution-focused principles and practices. Among the most striking results were increased student retention, improved test scores, and higher graduation rates.

The use of SFT techniques in a university counseling center setting is demonstrated in detail with an annotated transcript illustrating how SF Goal Development, SF Exception, and SF Scaling questions can be used to enhance academic performance and replace test anxiety with confidence.

EXPERIENTIAL EXERCISE: CREATING A CONFIDENCE SCALE

Think of a skill about which or a situation in which you would like to feel more confident and draw a 0–10 scale in which 10 represents Optimal Confidence and 0 represents Minimal Confidence.

Where would you rate yourself on the scale at this time?

What makes it that number?

What would it take to raise your number a half point, one point, two-points, etc.

Think of something that you could do in the next week that would raise your confidence about this skill or situation (even a little bit). Is this something you want to try?

REFERENCES

Beauchemin, J. D. (2018). Solution-focused wellness: A randomized controlled trial of college students. *Health & Social Work*, *43*(2), 94–100.

Berg, I. K., & Shilts. L. (2005). *Classroom solutions*. WOWW coaching. BFTC Press.

Brown, E. L., Powell, E., & Clark, A. (2012). Working on what works: Working with teachers to improve classroom behaviour and relationships. *Educational Psychology in Practice, 28*(1), 19–30.

Chen, H., Liu, X., Guz, S., Zhang, A., Franklin, C., Zhang, Y., & Qu, Y. (2018). The use of solution-focused brief therapy in Chinese schools: A qualitative analysis of practitioner perceptions. *International Journal of School Social Work, 3*(1), 239–270. 10.4148/2161-4148.1030.

Daki, J., & Savage, R. S. (2010). Solution-focused brief therapy: Impacts on academic and emotional difficulties. *The Journal of Educational Research, 103*(5), 309–326.

Fernie, L., & Cubeddu, D. (2016). WOWW: A solution orientated approach to enhance classroom relationships and behaviour within a primary three class. *Educational Psychology in Practice, 32*(2), 197–208.

Franklin, C., Guz, S., Zhang, A., Kim, J., Zheng, H., Hai, A. H., Cho, Y. J., & Shen, L. (2022). Solution-focused brief therapy for students in schools: A comparative meta-analysis of the US and Chinese literature. *Journal of the Society for Social Work and Research, 13*(2), 381–407.

Franklin, C., Montgomery, K. L., Baldwin, V, & Webb L. (2012). Research and development of a Solution-focused high school. In Cynthia Franklin, Terry S. Trepper, Wallace J. Gingerich, & Erick E. McCollum (Eds.), *Solution-focused brief therapy: A handbook of evidence-based practice.* New York: Oxford University Press, pp. 371–389.

Franklin, C., Streeter, C. L., Kim, J. S., & Tripodi, S. J. (2007). The effectiveness of a solution focused, public alternative school for dropout prevention and retrieval. *Children & Schools, 29,* 133–144.

Franklin, C., Streeter, C. L., Webbb, L., & Guz, S. (2018). *Solution focused brief therapy in alternative schools: Ensuring student success and dropout prevention.* New York, NY: Routledge.

Gillies, E. (2013). Solution focused approaches to promote effective home—school partnerships. In *School behaviour and families.* David Fulton Publishers, pp. 149–166.

Golmohamadi, M., & Kimiyaee, S. A. (2014). The effectiveness of group counseling based on solution-focused on academic motivation high school student with under achievement. *Research in Education, 1*(2), 55–62.

Huang, G., Li, H., & Li, F. (2014). The effect of solution focused group counseling on improving college students' academic procrastination. *China Journal of Health, 22*(11), 1708–1710.

Kelly, M. S., & Bluestone-Miller, R. (2009). Working on what works (WOWW): Coaching teachers to do more of what's working. *Children & Schools, 31*(1), 35–38. 10.1093/cs/31.1.35.

Kelly, M. S., Liscio, M., Bluestone-Miller, R., & Shilts, L. (2012). Making classrooms more solution- focused for teachers and students: The WOWW teacher coaching intervention. In C. Franklin, T. S. Trepper, W. J. Gingerich & E. E. McCollum (Eds.), *Solution-focused brief therapy: A handbook of evidence-based practice*. New York, NY, US: Oxford University Press, pp. 354–370.

Kim, J., Jordan, S. S., Franklin, C., & Froerer, A. (2019). Is solution-focused brief therapy evidence-based? An update 10 years later. *Families in Society: The Journal of Contemporary Social Services, 100,* 127–138.

Kim, J. S., Kelly, M. S., & Franklin, C. (2017). *Solution-focused brief therapy in schools: A 360 degree view of research and practice principles, 2nd Ed.* New York, NY: Oxford University Press.

Wallace, L. B., Hai, A. H., & Franklin, C. (2020). An evaluation of working on what works (WOWW): A solution-focused intervention for schools. *Journal of Marital and Family Therapy, 46*(4), 687–700.

Specific Programs and Interventions

Metcalf, L. (2008). *Counseling toward solutions: A practical solution-focused program for working with students, teachers, and parents, 2nd Ed.* New York: Jossey-Bass. http://www.wiley.com/WileyCDA/WileyTitle/productCd-0787998060.html

Websites

Garza Independence High School: A Solution-Focused High School. http://garzaindependencehs.weebly.com/solution-focused-approach.html.

Måhlberg, K., Sjöblom, M., & McKergow, M. Solution-focused education. sfwork.com/pdf/sfeducation.pdf.

Working on What Works: About the WOWW program; a solution-focused coaching method for schools: Video: https://youtu.be/zdOUyWTpUTc.

SOLUTION-FOCUSED THERAPY FOR TREATMENT OF POST-TRAUMATIC STRESS

The purpose of this chapter is to describe how SFT practitioners help people recover from post-traumatic stress symptoms (PTSD) that sometimes occur after experiencing emotionally or physically harmful or life threatening events. Such experiences might variously include natural disasters, domestic violence, rape, sexual or physical assault, bullying, or war combat experiences. The chapter begins with a description of the SF approach to trauma treatment, followed by case transcripts demonstrating SFT with survivors of physical assault, traumatic bereavement following a natural disaster, and being forced to flee from a war zone.

Known as post-traumatic stress disorder or PTSD, the primary constellation of symptoms occurring in the aftermath of traumatic events includes disturbing mental imagery or "flashbacks" and/or nightmares related to traumatic experiences, concentration difficulties, sadness, anger, fearfulness, difficulty relaxing, and/or feeling safe. PTSD is a serious disorder, with over 3% of the American population experiencing it over the last year and with a lifetime prevalence of about 7%. What contributes to PTSD being such a difficult disorder from a mental health perspective is that almost 40% of people suffering from PTSD have moderate or serious impairment (National Institute of Mental Health, 2023).

SFT AND PTSD

The main treatments for PTSD are psychotherapy, medication, or a combination of the two. In terms of psychotherapy, clinicians have

DOI: 10.4324/9781003401230-5

used a number of different approaches which help people identify and change troubling emotions, thoughts, and behaviors (National Institute of Mental Health, 2023). Interpersonal psychotherapy (cf Althobaiti et al., 2020), cognitive behavioral therapy (cf Roberts et al., 2015), and present-centered therapies such as mindfulness-based stress-reduction (e.g. Polusny et al., 2015) all have been shown to be effective for some people suffering from PTSD.

Although the research on SFT for the treatment of trauma is just beginning, these early studies suggest evidence of overall improvement for trauma survivors who received SFT, did not show evidence of harm from SFT, and showed that SFT was at least as effective as treatment-as-usual (Eads & Lee, 2019; Kim et al., 2021). In summarising the appropriateness of SFT for trauma treatment, Eads and Lee concluded:

> The application of SFT to trauma survivors draws from compelling conceptual arguments that a solution-focused approach could be an effective means of treating trauma without subjecting clients to the stress of directly focusing on traumatic memories. Notably, the included studies in this review did not show evidence of harms from SFT, and no evidence suggested SFT was less effective than TAU (treatment as usual). Furthermore, the benefits seen from SFT with trauma survivors on a variety of direct and indirect outcomes provide support for the systemic assumptions underlying the SFT treatment approach. The initial evidence supports the appropriateness of SFT for trauma survivors, and it is notable that SFT produced favorable treatment effects without a direct, past-focused approach to trauma treatment. Therefore, it is plausible that some of the clients who drop out of trauma-focused treatments could benefit from the SFT approach. (Eads & Lee, 2019, p. 8)

ADVANTAGES OF USING SFBT WITH PTSD

Stated most simply, SFT practitioners help people resolve the effects of painful life experiences associated with traumatic experiences by utilising clients' existing resources and strengths to create a satisfying and rewarding future that counterbalances and displaces post-traumatic symptoms. SF techniques are particularly well-suited to helping people recover from traumatic experiences because they help people cope, formulate, implement positive changes, and reclaim their quality of life after trauma by looking forward, not backward. Further, SF techniques are trauma-informed, hope-friendly, and future-focused (Rand & Cheavens, 2009).

Unlike most other psychotherapy approaches currently being used to treat trauma, which require clients to provide a descriptive history of their traumatic experiences, the SFT approach does not require people to excavate painful emotions or revisit traumatic past events in order to begin making positive changes. In the SFT approach it is the clients themselves who decide to what degree talking about specific details of the trauma will be healing and productive.

A further advantage of implementing the SF approach with traumatised people is that SFT techniques have a calming, soothing effect, foster positive emotions that interrupt upsetting thought patterns (von Cziffra-Bergs, 2018, p.57), and implicitly communicate a context of hope (Dolan, 1991, p. 40). Further, SFT can function as a natural counterbalance or "antidote" (Bannick, 2014, p. 7) to painful or disturbing feelings related to post-traumatic stress.

Like practitioners of most other approaches, SF practitioners also have the latitude to offer their clients additional resources when necessary. These might in some cases include medication, relaxation techniques, breathing techniques, self-help techniques, mindfulness meditation, yoga, or desensitisation protocols from problem-focused, technique-driven approaches like EMDR. Of the additional resources, yoga and mindfulness mediation are the most consistent with the SFBT approach because they provide relief by counterbalancing traumatic experiences and restoring present-focus.

However, it is important to remember that competent SFT practitioners do not offer resources outside the scope of SFT, for example desensitisation protocols, without first establishing a clear understanding of the specific details of the client's goal and fully exploring the already existing resources or "exceptions" within the client's behavioral repertoire, e.g. *Are there times when you might have had a panic attack or had trouble sleeping, but somehow managed not to? What's different about these times?*

While recognising that a variety of techniques derived from other approaches (relaxation, breathing and self-help techniques, meditation, yoga, desensitisation protocols) can sometimes be used to good effect within the SFT framework for trauma treatment when utilised collaboratively with the client, Steve de Shazer gave the following cautionary advice to aspiring SFT practitioners:

Any technique that requires a directive or expert stance on the part of that SF Practitioner or that compromises the client's ability to choose

> the direction of therapy is not compatible with the SFBT and should not be used if one wishes to maintain a solution-focused stance. (De Shazer et al., 2006, 2021, p. 160)

The unique way that SF practitioners typically approach relieving the suffering of trauma survivors is perhaps most clearly exemplified in the following conversation between the author and Insoo Kim Berg (Dolan, 2006), one of the primary developers of the SFT.[1]

> *Yvonne Dolan: Things are rarely the same for people after going through a traumatic experience.*
>
> *Insoo Kim Berg: That's right – But it's important to remember that it's not only bad things that change people's lives. Good things that happen can also result in profound changes, particularly if we learn to pay attention to them. Falling in love, having a baby or a grandchild, going to school, getting a job – all these things can have major impacts. It is important to help people focus on what motivates them to carry on with life.*
>
> *YD: I've known people who have lost almost everything, but then somehow they manage to go on in order to care for their child, for the sake of a loved one, a pet, a cause that they deeply believe in such as fighting for their country's freedom, saving others, things like that …*
>
> *IKB: Exactly: They somehow find a way to carry on, and eventually one thing leads to another, some time passes and things gradually become better or at the very least, more bearable. But positive changes can only happen in the present and future. Focusing on the past rarely makes things better.*
>
> *YD: What about clients telling an SF Practitioner about what happened?*
>
> *IKB: If the client feels that talking about what happened will be helpful, we should definitely encourage and support them in talking about it to whatever degree is helpful, and of course respond to them with empathy and compassion. But people should not be required to mentally revisit painful events unless they think it will be helpful, in some way. It is important to remember that this is not the same for every person. In some cultures, Korea for example, being required to disclose the details of traumatic experience can actually make things worse because; being required to talk about it to a relative stranger can in some cases be nearly as traumatic as the event itself. We need to respect our clients' expertise about their needs and goals and the best way for us to support them in moving forward.*

---

[1] To further contextualise this conversation, it should be noted that Berg and Dolan had both personally experienced trauma and its effects. Berg was a Korean War survivor, Dolan had survived childhood sexual and physical abuse, and both had endured the traumatic loss of loved ones in the Korean War.

> YD: *One of the primary goals I hear survivors express is that they want to spend less time thinking about the traumatic experience and more time focusing on the present and future.*
>
> IKB: *Yes, and that needs to be respected. In the SF approach, it is always the client who determines the course of therapy.*

As Berg emphasised, it is always the client's goals that ultimately determine what happens in an SFT session. When working with a survivor who expresses that it would be helpful to talk about the details of a traumatic event, SFT practitioners begin by exploring how the client's hopes for how it will be helpful. Identifying a goal based on the clients' best hopes provides an important reference point that can help them to stay oriented to the present while telling the story. This can be especially important for maintaining a sense of psychological safety while describing emotionally painful past experiences.

The SFT approach does not require people to excavate painful emotions or revisit traumatic past events in order to begin making positive changes. Typical goals that survivors identify for telling the story of their traumatic experiences include:

> *I won't feel so alone with the memory.*
>
> *I will stop constantly blaming myself.*
>
> *I will begin to move on with my life.*

When a client describes the traumatic experience, it is only natural for the SF practitioner to express compassion, e.g. *I am so very sorry that this happened to you.* But more is usually needed. Recognising that even the most carefully chosen words can sometimes be completely inadequate in response to horrifically painful traumatic experiences, practitioners trained in the SF approach to treatment of trauma do not shy away from directly acknowledging the relative inadequacy of language in the face of complex traumatic experiences (Dolan, 1991, Kim & Froerer, 2018), for example:

> *I think that there are likely no words that can adequately express how painful (terrible) this must have been for you and how difficult this has been.*

In summary, the SF approach is uniquely appropriate for alleviating the effects of traumatic experiences because it is implicitly and consistently future-focused and goal oriented and serves to generate client behaviors that naturally serve to counterbalance and displace painful past experiences.

HOW IS SFT SPECIFICALLY UTILISED TO TREAT TRAUMA?

SF practitioners approach treating PTSD in much the same way that they approach other kinds of solution development: They generate a detailed description of what the client's life will be like when things are better, or at the very least, sufficiently navigable and reasonably satisfying based on the client's unique personal needs, preferences, and circumstances.

Not surprisingly, people coping with the aftermath of trauma oftentimes find it initially easier to describe what they do not want to continue (intrusive memories, insomnia, flashbacks, chaos) than what they want to have happen and find it helpful to be asked what they want "instead." These descriptions are then utilised to generate specific goals and reveal specific behaviors that the client can begin implementing in order to move in the direction of a uniquely personalised description of what "better" looks like.

SF practitioners work with traumatised people in much the same way that they implement the SFT approach in other contexts. Once the client's immediate goal(s) have been clearly identified, they are offered SF Scaling Questions to quickly assess the current distance from the goal and SF Exception Questions to identify helpful behaviors (exceptions) already present or potentially present in the client's life. Oftentimes, clients may have naturally begun implementing at least some helpful coping behaviors on their own or they can identify previous behaviors that will prove helpful to resume in order to move forward in the desired direction of feeling better. SF **Scaling Questions** and **SF Exception Question**s are offered throughout the SF trauma treatment process.

Although offering SF scaling questions in the aftermath of trauma might initially appear counterintuitive, their role in effective trauma treatment is important. Obviously, with SF Scaling and all other SF techniques, the SF practitioner's sensitivity to timing and appropriateness in relation to the client's current emotional state is essential. For example, abruptly introducing an SF Scale when someone is in tears would not only be emotionally insensitive and most likely counterproductive; it would also reflect an erroneous understanding of the inherently respectful, client-centered nature of the SF approach.

When introducing a scaling question to a trauma survivor, SF practitioners typically explain its purpose and ask permission beforehand. When the reason for offering a scaling question is respectfully explained and offered with sensitivity, trauma survivors typically respond positively. Once they have been introduced, **SF Scaling Questions** can simultaneously function as an emotion-calming solution-development resource and an ongoing assessment tool to ensure that treatment is going in the right direction in relation to the client's immediate needs and ongoing goals. Further, clients sometimes find it helpful to utilise SF scaling on their own as a self-help resource in between SF sessions and after treatment ends.

Although the precise content of every SF session is necessarily unique to the client being served, the following case exemplifies what a typical SF session looks like when the SF approach is utilised to help a person experiencing PTSD related to a recent traumatic experience.

CASE EXAMPLE: JOE – *I NEED HELP DEALING WITH WHAT HAPPENED TO ME*[2]

A young electrician employed by a large electrical contracting firm, Joe had recently survived a violent, potentially life threatening physical attack. Returning to his parked truck at the end of the work day, he had been approached by two men who violently beat him up and stole his wallet. Although badly bruised, Joe somehow managed to drive home afterwards. But that night he had trouble sleeping, and subsequently became increasingly anxious and apprehensive about returning to work.

Joe's boss was initially understanding about Joe taking a few days off from work to recover from the incident. But after Joe misses work for three consecutive weeks, his boss insists that he schedule an appointment with mental health professional.

---

[2]The reader may notice that this chapter's case transcripts are somewhat more heavily annotated than previous chapter. The additional annotations are intended to reveal the particularly nuanced use of language that oftentimes characterises skilled SFT practitioners work with traumatised clients.

Joe's Solution-Focused Sessions

The solution-focused practitioner greets Joe in a friendly fashion. After exchanging pleasantries and taking a few moments to get acquainted[3], he asks Joe to describe what needs to happen as a result of today's session in order to be able to honestly say afterwards that it had proved helpful:

Solution-Focused Practitioner: What will need to happen as a result of coming here in order for you to be able to honestly say afterwards that it had been helpful to come today? **(SF Goal Development Question).**

Joe: I would be able to go back to work. I got attacked by two guys last month when I was leaving a construction site at the end of the day. I was there doing some electrical work – I am an electrician. They ambushed me and beat me up, cracked two of my ribs, and stole my wallet. It really shook me up. I haven't been back to work since.

Solution-Focused Practitioner: That must have been a terrifying experience – I am so very sorry to hear that happened to you! Would it be helpful to talk more about what happened to you before we talk about your getting back to work? **(SF Goal Development Question).**

Joe: No, I don't think so now that I've told you what happened. The main thing is that I need to get back to work before I lose my job. I have a wife and two kids to support.

Solution-Focused Practitioner: The main thing is getting back to work. You sound really motivated to do that. **(SF Direct Compliment).**

Joe: (He nods). I am tired of worrying about not going into the office. **(SF Detail Question).**

Solution-Focused Practitioner: Let's suppose that you start going into the office again – what difference will that make for you?

Joe: I won't be laying awake half the night worrying about the money I am losing because I am not working. I wouldn't wake up in a bad mood and be cranky with my wife and kids.

Solution-Focused Practitioner: What will you be doing instead of laying awake half the night and being cranky in the morning? **(SF Instead Question).**

Joe: I would wake up in a good mood. I would probably kiss my wife, get up and make some coffee, and go into my sons' room to wake them up in a nice

---

[3]SF practitioners oftentimes routinely take a few moments at the beginning of each session to "join with the client" by talking about an everyday topic unrelated to the client's reason for coming such as the weather, local events, etc. This can be particularly useful when working with someone who has been experiencing anxiety associated with PTSD, as it can in some cases help them to relax in order to be able to actively participate in the session.

way instead of just yelling at them from the kitchen to get their butts out of bed. And I then I would leave for work.

Solution-Focused Practitioner: Let's suppose you do those things. How will your wife and kids likely react? **(SF Detail Question).**

Joe: Everyone will be in a more positive mood. Right now we are all on edge. My wife is afraid I am going to lose my job.

Solution-Focused Practitioner: And how do you imagine people at your work will react? **(SF Detail Question).**

Joe: Everyone will be happy to see me. We're short staffed at the moment. Usually we all show up at the office at 7:30 am to pick up our assignments for the day. Everyone gets themselves a coffee and then we all leave again to do whatever contracts we were assigned.

Solution-Focused Practitioner: Is there anything else that will be different? **(SF Is There Anything Else Question).**

Joe: No, not really. Those are the main things.

Solution-Focused Practitioner: You have given me a nice clear description of what you want to have happen. **(SF Direct Compliment).** *Is it okay if I draw a little scale to help me better understand what will be most helpful?*[4]

Joe: Okay.

Solution-Focused Practitioner: (He draws a horizontal line on a piece of paper with a 0 at one end of the line and 10 at the other end with *Back at Work* written above the 10 and *The Opposite* over the zero.

०———————————————————————————————10

He then hands Joe a pencil)

Let's imagine that the 10 represents your being comfortably back at work with all the good things that go with that and 0 represents just the opposite of that. Please make a mark on the scale to show where you are now. **(SF Scaling Question).**

Joe: Okay. (Joe takes the pen and after a brief pause makes a small vertical mark approximately one-third of the way across the horizontal scale).

Solution-Focused Practitioner: Great. What number should we call that? **(SF Scaling Question).**

Joe: It is something like a 3 1/2.

Solution-Focused Practitioner: What makes it a 3 and a 1/2 and not for example, a 3? **(SF Scaling Question).**

Joe: Well … . I guess it would be the fact that I still have a job, things are at least for now still going pretty much ok between me and my wife, and I have two great kids. And some nights I sleep a little better than others.

---

[4]Notice how the SF practitioner explains the purpose of the scale and respectfully asks permission before introducing it.

Solution-Focused Practitioner: I noticed that you said you sleep better some nights. What's different about the nights you sleep better? **(SF Exception Question).**

Joe: On mornings after I've managed to sleep a little better, I feel less grumpy. That's the only thing I can think of ...

Solution-Focused Practitioner: Would the number be a little higher on those mornings when you have slept better and are feeling less grumpy? **(SF Scaling Question).**

Joe: I guess it would be more like a 4 1/2 on those days.

Solution-Focused Practitioner: That is very interesting. At a 4 1/2 you are almost halfway toward your goal. Is there anything else that is different **(SF Difference Question)** *on those days that you are at a 4 and 1/2?* **(SF Scaling Question).**

Joe: (He pauses, obviously thinking). *I suppose that on those days that I managed to go to bed more relaxed and less worried that something bad might happen to me again the next time I went to work.*

Solution-Focused Practitioner: What do you think helped you be more relaxed on those days? **(SF Coping Question).**

Joe: It helps if I get some physical exercise, so playing basketball outside with my 2 sons has been good even if I am still a little bit stiff where I was bruised.

Solution-Focused Practitioner: What else helps? **(SF What Else Question).**

Joe: It helps if I have something already planned for the next day when I go to bed at night.

SF Practitioner: How is that helpful? **(SF Exception Question).**

Joe: Sometimes when I am about to go to sleep I find myself remembering what happened. It helps to have something else to focus on when my mind starts going in that direction.

SF Practitioner: When your mind starts reliving what happened, it helps to refocus in the direction of what you have planned for the next day? **(SF Exception Question).**

Joe: Yes, it helps a lot. Otherwise I can start reliving what happened in my mind and my heart starts racing and I get freaked out.

SF Practitioner: Wow. How did you figure out to do that?[5] **(SF Indirect Compliment).**

Joe: It just seems normal to focus on what I have planned for the next day if in fact I have plans for the next day.

SF Practitioner: Let's suppose you start having those thoughts about what happened to you, sort of reliving it, and your heart starts aching but you don't have plans for the next day. What helps then? **(SF Coping Question).**

---

[5]Joe has described an important SF Exception to the problem. This also illustrates how having a future-focus can serve to counterbalance intrusive thoughts about past trauma.

Joe: It helps if I do something to distract myself like getting out of bed, walking downstairs, getting a glass of water, or turning on the TV. It seems to help if I physically move. It's like it breaks the pattern of thinking about what happened.

SF Practitioner: So let's suppose you do that, you go downstairs, get a drink of water, or watch some TV, what happens next? **(SF Question).**

Joe: It's like my mind returns to normal.

SF Practitioner: Have you used this way of refocusing you mind and getting back to normal in other situations after going through something like this? **(SF Detail Question).**

Joe: I used to do something like that at others times when I was upset about something and I needed to calm down. It helps to walk around as a way to clear your mind and refocus. I've seen sports coaches do that with players and the players doing it themselves when they are upset about a bad call from one of the umpires. They call it 'walking it off.'

SF Practitioner: And this works well for you? **(SF Coping Question).**

Joe: It does.

SF Practitioner: Is there anything else you've found that helps when something like that happens and you start revisiting what happened?

Joe: Basically, thinking about what I am going to do the next day, or doing something physical that snaps me into the present and makes me pay attention to what I am doing.

SF Practitioner: How did you learn to do this? **(SF Indirect Compliment).**

Joe: It was survival I guess. Bad things happen and you have to go on afterwards and do what you need to do.

SF Practitioner: Does it feel sufficient for you, doing things that redirect your focus to the present at times when these memories come up? **(SF Coping Question).** I'm asking this because there are other things that might possibly help that we could talk about if you think that would be helpful.

Joe: No, I think what I am doing is working, so it feels sufficient at least for now. And the memories of what happened that night are starting to come up less frequently as time goes by.[6]

Solution-Focused Practitioner: I am impressed that you already found several things that helped before you came here.[7] **(SF Direct Compliment).**

Joe: Thanks.

Solution-Focused Practitioner: Is there anything else that has helped you to relax and sleep better so as to wake at a 4 and 1/2? **(SF What Else Question).**

---

[6] If Joe had expressed that it was not sufficient and that he needed something more, the SF practitioner could have offered the possibility of various specific desensitisation techniques such as EMDR.

[7] SF practitioners are attentive to the fact that clients oftentimes independently discover their own unique ways to make things better prior to coming to therapy.

Joe: My wife has been very understanding and that really makes a difference.

Solution-Focused Practitioner: It helped that she was nice and understanding.

Joe: Yes, I guess I was worried that she would think I was being weak because I had been afraid to go back to work.

Solution-Focused Practitioner: How was it helpful to you that she reacted in an understanding way?

Joe: I felt that she believed in me, and that had an encouraging effect on me.

Solution-Focused Practitioner: I find it very interesting that you use the word 'encouraging' to describe the effect of your wife believing in you. It occurs to me that the word 'encourage' contains the word, 'courage.' Does this perhaps mean[8] that your wife's believing in you is helping you find some of the courage necessary to go back to work?

Joe: Yes, I think that is true.

Solution-Focused Practitioner: What do you think has helped you find courage to go forward at other times **(SF Exception Question)** in your life when things were challenging or hard?

Joe: When I was kid, my mother and I lived for several years with a mean, nasty drunk guy who stayed at home all day and didn't go to work. He was my mother's boyfriend and he owned the house we were living in. He yelled at me all the time and told me I would never amount to anything. But I ignored him and went to school every day and went to work after school too because I didn't want to be around him and I didn't want to be like him.

Solution-Focused Practitioner: Living with him must have been difficult.

Joe: It was. But if I left I knew that my mother would be all alone with him, and I wouldn't have a place to live.

Solution-Focused Practitioner: So you found the strength and courage to stay there even though it was hard and you kept going to school and going to work too?

Joe: I did. I finished high school and started taking classes so I could eventually qualify for my electrician's license.

Solution-Focused Practitioner: You went through a lot but you kept persevering. Very impressive. **(SF Direct Compliment)**. How did you manage to do that? **(SF Indirect Compliment)**.

Joe: I did it for my Mom as well as for myself. After I got my electrician's license I started making more money and I was able to move out and get my own place. My Mom asked if she could move in with me. I knew it was the only way she was going to be able to leave that jerk she was living with so I said yes even though I knew it was going to be hard for me to share such a small place with her. She lived with me for almost a year until she

---

[8]SF practitioners deliberately refrain from making interpretations, instead inviting their clients to describe the meaning of behaviors and words as exemplified here.

had saved up enough money to put down a rent deposit on her own place. She still lives there.

Solution-Focused Practitioner: You clearly really helped her. She must be very proud of you. **(SF Direct Compliment).**

Joe: I think she is.

Solution-Focused Practitioner: Is there anything else that goes with that 4 and 1/2? **(SF Scaling Question).**

Joe: I can't think of anything.

Solution-Focused Practitioner: In that case, is it okay if I ask you another question? This one requires quite a bit of imagination.[9]

Joe: Okay.

Solution-Focused Practitioner: I would like you to imagine that one night you fall asleep and that sometime in the middle of the night while you and your wife are sleeping very peacefully something remarkable happens, a sort of miracle in which suddenly you have moved up to a 10 on your scale. But of course neither you nor your wife knows that this has happened because you have been asleep. What do you think will be the first thing that you or she will notice that is different the next morning that will tell you that you are now at a 10? **(Miracle Question).**

Joe: I don't know ... (he pauses). 'I guess the first thing is I would wake up with a smile on my face.

Solution-Focused Practitioner: Would your wife notice this?

Joe: No, she would probably be still asleep. I am usually the first one to get up.

Solution-Focused Practitioner: What would happen next on this miracle day?

Joe: I would probably go into the kitchen, start the coffee, and then go wake the boys up.

Solution-Focused Practitioner: What would they notice?

Joe: They'd notice that Dad was back to his normal self.

Solution-Focused Practitioner: What would that look like?[10]

Joe: I'd be joking around with them, telling them it was time to come and eat breakfast.

Solution-Focused Practitioner: How would they respond?[11]

---

[9]Notice how the SF Practitioner asks permission before asking the Miracle Question and explains that it will require some imagination.

[10]Asking what something will *look like* invites a specific behavioral description that will likely subsequently prove easier for the client to replicate as opposed to a description of what it will *feel* like.

[11]Asking clients to imagine how they and other people in their life would react to the "miracle" creates a virtual mental rehearsal for the behavioral changes the client associates with things getting better. This then creates the possibility for the client to subsequently deliberately replicate portions of the identified behavior in order to move in the direction of the desired change or goal.

Joe: They would ask for toaster waffles. They always want toaster waffles. And I would make them for their breakfast.

Solution-Focused Practitioner: What would happen next?

Joe: I'd make their waffles and then drink some coffee. Then my wife would come into the kitchen and I would tell her good morning and then I would go get ready for work.

Solution-Focused Practitioner: How would your wife react to this?

Joe: She would be happy because she would know that I was going to work that day which meant that things were going to be ok.

Solution-Focused Practitioner: What would she do that would tell you that she was happy?

Joe: She would smile at me and give me a kiss before I left.

Solution-Focused Practitioner: How would you react to that?

Joe: I would kiss her back and then drive to work feeling pretty good.

Solution-Focused Practitioner: What happens next on this Miracle day?

Joe: I show up at work, say hello to my co-workers and pick up my work assignment for that day from my boss.

Solution-Focused Practitioner: How will[12] they likely react?

Joe: Everyone would be happy to see me. They might make a few jokes or talk about some of the sports teams we all follow. My boss would probably pat me on the back. He is that kind of guy,

Solution-Focused Practitioner: What happens next?

Joe: I go wherever I need to go and do my work for the day. Then I come home and eat dinner with my wife and kids. We have a nice night and eventually I go to bed and have a good sleep.

Solution-Focused Practitioner: Sounds like a nice day.

Joe: It would be. It's what I want.

Solution-Focused Practitioner: You clearly know what you want and what needs to happen.

Joe: Yes, I do.

Solution-Focused Practitioner: Can I ask you another scaling question? **(SF Scaling Question).**

Joe: Okay.

Solution-Focused Practitioner: Imagine a scale in which 10 represents that you feel completely confident that you will be able to achieve that Miracle you just described and 0 means just the opposite, that you have

---

[12]The SF practitioner's deliberate choice of the word *will* (rather than *would*) invites the client to experience a sort of virtual rehearsal. This is a good example of the careful attention to language that is inherent in the SF approach and consistently characterises its most skilled ongoing use by advanced SF practitioners.

no confidence that you will be able to do it. Where are you right now in terms of that confidence? **(SF Scaling Question).**

Joe: In terms of confidence, I would say that I am at an 8 or a 9. In order to be at a 10, I would have to be actually back at work.

Solution-Focused Practitioner: That makes sense. What makes your confidence an 8 or 9? **(SF Scaling Question).**

Joe: I really care about my family and I know they are depending on me. They are the reason I need to go back to work.

Solution-Focused Practitioner: The fact that your family is depending on you motivates and makes you want to go back to work and that puts you at an 8 or 9 in confidence that you can do it? **(SF Scaling Question).**

Joe: Yes.

Solution-Focused Practitioner: Ok, here is one more scaling question. Imagine another scale between 0–10 in which 10 means you are willing to literally do anything necessary in order to go back to work, and 0 means just the opposite. **(SF Scaling Question).**

Joe: Pretty high. At least a 9. I'm a tough guy.

Solution-Focused Practitioner: I believe you. You clearly are a strong person. **(SF Direct Compliment).**

Joe: Thanks.

Solution-Focused Practitioner: Okay, before we move on, is there anything else I should have asked or that you think might be important for us to talk about today? **(SF Safety Net Question).**

Joe: No, I don't think so.

Solution-Focused Practitioner: In that case, assuming it is okay with you, I would like just take a moment to offer you a few thoughts. (Joe nods).

I think you have done a very good job of figuring things out, and I am also impressed by what a caring father and husband you are, the kind of guy who talks things over with his wife, respects what she has to say about things, and the kind of father who makes waffles for his kids. **(SF Direct Compliment).**

Between now and the next time we meet, assuming you want to come back for another session, I would like you to continue to to pay attention[13] to anything that you or anyone else in your life does that helps you find the courage you need to move in the direction of the 10. Meanwhile, I would also like you to invite you to try experimenting with doing the various

---

[13]"I would like you to pay attention" exemplifies the SF stance of allowing the client rather than the SF practitioner to decide what fits best for them and is most likely to help them accomplish their goals. Although the practitioner would "like" the client to do something, the choice about whether to do so is always ultimately up to the client.

things you described that help you to relax like getting physical exercise, talking with your wife, enjoying dinner with your family.[14]

Joe: I will give that a try.

Session Ends.

Joe's Next Session

Solution-Focused Practitioner: How are things going— what's better? **(SF What's Better Question).**

Joe: I guess we could say that I am at a 10. I've been back at work on Monday. But I am still experiencing a lot of anxiety thinking about whether I will be safe returning to my truck at the end of the day.

Solution-Focused Practitioner: I think that is of course completely understandable, but before we move on to talking about the safety concern, I don't want to lose track of the fact that you managed to go back to work. How many days did you manage to work this week?

Joe: Every day.

Solution-Focused Practitioner: Every day!! How did you do manage to do this? **(SF Indirect Compliment).**

Joe: I was definitely motivated. My wife and I live paycheck to paycheck; we need my paycheck for everyday necessities like buying groceries and rent so we can keep a roof over our heads. I had already used up almost all of my sick time allowance from work, and on top of that we were already behind in fulfilling our contracts with several of the home builders we work with on a regular basis.

Solution-Focused Practitioner: So you had some pressure on both sides to get back to work?

Joe: I did.

Solution-Focused Practitioner: Some people might have caved in under that kind of pressure coming on top of experiencing such a traumatic experience just a couple of weeks ago. How did you find the strength to come back to work despite perhaps feeling a bit pressured both by the demands of the job and the necessity of generating money to support your family?

Joe: Well, like I told you before, I am a tough guy. I grew up the hard way. If I wanted something I had to do it myself, make things happen for myself.

Solution-Focused Practitioner: And you grew up to become the kind of man who does things for himself and takes care of his family. **(SF Direct Compliment).** *Is that also part of your finding this strength?*

Joe: Absolutely. I really care about my family. I don't want my kids to grow up the way I did.

---

[14]This is an example of inviting the client to try an SF "experiment."

Solution-Focused Practitioner: It is obvious that you are not only a tough, strong guy but also a man who really cares about his kids. (**SF Direct Compliment**).
Joe: I do. Any my wife, too.
Solution-Focused Practitioner: And your wife too. Is your wife also part of that strength you have, the strength to go back to work even though it was clearly not an easy thing to do?
Joe: Yes, definitely my wife.
Solution-Focused Practitioner: Your wife also is part of that strength. So, given that you are back at work, what would be the most important thing for us to focus on today in order for it to have been useful for you? (**SF Goal Development Question**).
Joe: I don't know ... I'd like to feel less anxious.
Solution-Focused Practitioner: You'd like to feel less anxious. What would you like to be feeling instead of anxiety?
Joe: I guess I would be feeling relaxed, but actually, not too relaxed because I work with electricity so I really need to focus on what I am doing. You can really get hurt if you mess up with an electrical current. I have heard of people literally being knocked off a high ladder and breaking bones.
Solution-Focused Practitioner: So you want to be relaxed but also able to focus as alertly as you need to depending on what you are doing? (**SF Goal Development Question**).
Joe: Yes, that sounds about right. Alert, but not anxious, not spending all day thinking about whether I will be safe when I go back to the truck.
Solution-Focused Practitioner: It sounds like safety is part of this, too? (**SF Goal Development Question**).
Joe: Actually, safety is the most important thing right now. If I knew I was going to be safe going back to my truck at the end of the day, I wouldn't be worried, I wouldn't feel anxious all day while I am working.
Solution-Focused Practitioner: What would you be feeling instead? (**SF Instead Question**).
Joe: Comfortable and alert. Like I normally did both on the job and at home, although sometimes I am more relaxed at home because I do need the same level of focus when I am not working with electrical circuits and breakers.
Solution-Focused Practitioner: I think I understand. Is it okay if I draw[15] a scale?
Joe: Okay.
Solution-Focused Practitioner: Let's imagine a 0–10 scale in which 10 signifies you knowing without a doubt that you will be safe when you go to

---

[15]SF practitioners sometimes draw the scale and other times simply describe it. Sometimes drawing a literal scale serves to make it feel more "real" to the client and makes it easier for them to answer scaling questions associated with it. When working with trauma survivors, drawing a literal scale can serve to further concretise the concept of personal safety.

your truck at the end of the day, and o represents just the opposite: You wouldn't even think of going to work. (The SF practitioner now takes a piece of paper and draws a horizontal line with o on the far left end and 10 on the far right end with the words Dangerous, not going to work written over the o and Safe written over the 10).

o_____10

Where would you say you are on the scale right now? (He gives the paper with the scale on it to Joe and hands him pen).

Joe: (He sits motionless for a moment, looking at the paper). *The problem here is life is uncertain. Nothing is ever entirely safe. Bad things happen every day. So it really isn't reasonable to assume that any place is completely safe.*

Solution-Focused Practitioner: You are absolutely right. How about it we call the 10 Reasonably Safe instead of Safe?

(He gestures for Joe to give the paper back, changes the wording above the 10 to read, Reasonably Safe, and hands it back to Joe). *Where would you say you are on this version of the scale?* **(SF Scaling Question).**

Joe: Most of the time I would say I am close to a 10. Certainly at home I usually at a 10. It would be a little lower when I am driving — I mean the traffic is crazy out there somedays — maybe a 9. At work it's something like an 8 because I am working with electricity. And it's a little bit lower than that if I am working on a job in a neighborhood that I don't know very well or one that has a reputation for being dangerous. In that situation it is more like a 6.

Solution-Focused Practitioner: That makes sense. Let's take all that into account. (The SF Practitioner now adds up the numbers to obtain an average). *If we average all those numbers together, we get 8 and 1/4. Is that where you would put yourself on this scale?* **(SF Scaling Question).**

Joe: It's actually higher than I thought, but I feel like it needs to be better when I am at work. It feels like the safety level is already good enough at home and when I am driving, it's really just at work.

Solution-Focused Practitioner: So the only portion of your life where it is not yet good enough is at work? It is already ok in the other situations?

Joe: Yes.

Solution-Focused Practitioner: Let's adjust the scale again. (He crosses out the previous words written over the 10, writes Reasonably Safe at Work, and returns the paper to Joe). *Make a mark to represent how safe you feel at work this week.* **(SF Scaling Question).**

Joe: (He marks the paper). *If 10 means reasonably safe, I would put it at a 7 1/2 at work overall. Because I don't always know ahead of time what I am walking into in terms of the neighborhood.*

Solution-Focused Practitioner: Of course. What do you think would help make it a little bit higher? **(SF Scaling Question).**

Joe: If I knew more about the different neighborhoods in the city that would help because I would know more of what to expect.

Solution-Focused Practitioner: That makes sense. Let's suppose you got to know more or less what to expect in all the different areas of the city. How would that effect your position on the scale? **(SF Scaling Question).**

Joe: I think that would make it pretty close to a 10.

Solution-Focused Practitioner: Is there anything else that you need to do or that would help?

Joe: I am pretty sure that I know what to do to get more familiar with the city, but I am also thinking that maybe it would help if I looked into some other work possibilities where the place or places I would be working were more predictable. There are building maintenance companies for example that are always looking for electricians.

Solution-Focused Practitioner: Do you think it might be helpful to explore those options, too?

Joe: I do.

Solution-Focused Practitioner: It sounds like you have made a really good analysis of the situation. **(SF Direct Compliment).**

Joe: Thanks, I think I have.

Solution-Focused Practitioner: Is there anything else that would help further solidify or maintain that 10 on the scale? **(SF Scaling Question).**

Joe: I think it will also help for some time to pass. I still have some visible bruises when I take off my shirt. Every time I look in the mirror and see the bruises it brings it all back. That is not easy.

Solution-Focused Practitioner: Of course. And you are looking forward to a time when you do not see those bruises anymore, when they have healed?

Joe: Yes, and then I won't be thinking about what happened to me that night.

Solution-Focused Practitioner: What will you be thinking about instead? [16] **(SF Instead Question).**

Joe: I'll be thinking about other things, what I am planning to do over the weekend, things like that, or maybe what a good looking guy I am seeing in the mirror. (He laughs).

Solution-Focused Practitioner: Sounds like positive things.

Joe: Definitely.

Solution-Focused Practitioner: So time passing is going to help. Is there anything else that you think would be helpful to talk about? **(SF Safety Net Question).**

---

[16]Notice how the SFT practitioner moves Joe from describing what he *does not* want to be thinking to asking what he will be thinking about *instead* when the bruises are gone. The Instead Question is used to help a client change a negative goal (what *will not* occur) to a positive one (what *will* occur).

Joe: No, I feel like I have a pretty good idea of what I need to do.
Solution-Focused Practitioner: You know what to do.
Joe: Yes, definitely.
Solution-Focused Practitioner: You sound very clear about this.
Joe: I am. I feel confident that I know how to move forward again. But can I call you in the future for another appointment if something else happens and I start having trouble again?
Solution-Focused Practitioner: Absolutely. I think you have made a very good plan. **(SF Direct Compliment).**
Joe: Thanks, I feel good about it.

SESSION ENDS

DISCUSSION

Beginning with their first meeting, the SFT practitioner's questions implicitly communicated confidence that Joe knew what would signify that things things were better and would be able to figure out how to begin moving in that direction if asked the right questions. In the first session, this meant that Joe would be able to go back to work, and in the second session, this meant becoming more familiar with the city, looking into job alternatives, and allowing some time to pass so that his body could further heal.

Notice how before the sessions end, the SFT practitioner asks if there is anything else on which they should focus. This **SF Safety Net Question** is a way to both ensure that clients' problems have been adequately addressed and give them the opportunity to bring up any additional issues that might be troubling them.

Although the SF Practitioner makes it clear that Joe is welcome to return for additional sessions, the choice is clearly left up to Joe. Again, SF practitioners assume that their clients are the best experts on their own lives, what changes need to happen in order for them to know that they are moving forward in the right direction, and by extension, whether they need further SFT sessions.

CASE EXAMPLE: PETER – SFT FOLLOWING A TRAUMATIC LOSS

Peter's community was recently ravaged by a powerful earthquake that destroyed the apartment building where he lived with his wife and children. The SF practitioner is a volunteer sent by a local charity to offer support to people who have lost loved ones as a result of the disaster.

The SF practitioner begins by exchanging pleasantries with Peter and then moves on to asking what will need to happen as a result of the session in order for it to prove helpful.

SF Practitioner: What needs to happen as a result of our meeting today in order for you to feel afterwards that it was helpful and not a waste of your time? **(SF Goal Development Question).**

Peter: The most immediate thing is that I need to get through the next few days and do the best job possible continuing to take care of my seven year old son while also making plans for the burial of my wife and daughters. I don't even know where to start. Our apartment building collapsed and my wife and my two little girls died instantly in the explosion.

SF Practitioner: I am so very sorry! I cannot even begin to imagine how painful and difficult this must be for you.

Peter: You really can't. No one can.

SF Practitioner: I am sure that it hurts far more and is much more difficult than any words could ever describe.[17]

Peter: It really does.

SF Practitioner: I am so very sorry. (Brief, respectful pause). I want to do my best to help in whatever way I can. There is a simple diagram I sometimes use to help me better understand how I can best be helpful in situations like this. Is it ok if I draw a line on a piece of paper?[18]

Peter: Okay.

SF Practitioner: (Draws a scale).

o_____10

Let's imagine that 10 represents the point in time when you have completed the burial and you have also continued to take good care of your son and in both cases you have done the best job possible under the circumstances and o represents the Opposite.[19]

---

[17]Notice that although the SF practitioner expresses sympathy and acknowledges the inadequacy of words to express the extreme level of pain the client is experiencing, he deliberately continues to respectfully focus on the client's goal.

[18]Explaining the reason for drawing the SF scale and respectfully asking permission beforehand is especially important in situations like Peter's because (in the author's longtime experience) people who have experienced recent trauma understandably tend to dislike surprises and unpredictability. When done with sensitivity and respect, however, answering a scaling question gently moderates and counterbalances painful emotions by causing the person to naturally access the part of the brain associated with evaluative thinking.

[19]The "Opposite" serves to represent what the client does not want or likely fears without unnecessarily requiring them to go through the painful process of describing what they do not want to have happen.

Peter. (Nods).

SF Practitioner. (Hands Peter a pencil and the piece of paper with the scale on it).

I'd like you to make a mark on the line to represent where you are now.

Peter. (He marks a point at approximately the 2 position).

SF Practitioner. You have already been through so much and yet somehow you have managed to be at a 2 today – what makes it a 2 and not lower? **(SF Scaling Question).**

Peter. I have managed to make sure that my little boy has gotten something to eat every morning and every night and I have managed to arrange for us to stay with my cousin so that we have a warm place to sleep now that our apartment building no longer exists.

SF Practitioner. And those things make it a 2. Is there anything else that contributes to the 2?

Peter. My cousin's wife and children have been very kind to us and very welcoming.

SF Practitioner. And that also has contributed to the 2? **(SF Scaling Question).**

Peter. Yes, I don't know what we would have done without them.

SF Practitioner. And you really appreciate that.

Peter. I am very grateful we were able to make our way to their village.

SF Practitioner. I have a feeling that you are the kind of person who would have done the same for them if they were in your situation. **(SF Direct Compliment).**

Peter. Yes, I would.

SF Practitioner. What will be the next thing that will need to happen in order for you to move higher on the scale? **(SF Scaling Question).**

Peter. (After a short pause and a deep breathe) I will need to find a place with electricity where I can charge my cell phone and then I will need to contact the authorities to get permission to make arrangements for the burials.

SF Practitioner. Let's suppose that you manage to get your phone charged up again and you contact the authorities and get permission, what number would that be on the scale?

Peter. I think that will make it a 4.

SF Practitioner. A 4. And what will be going on with your son at a 4? **(SF Scaling Question).**

Peter. I will continue to see that he has food to eat and that he is safe and I will make sure he is never alone. My cousin and his wife will help with that. And I will need to somehow find both him and me some clean clothes to wear to the funeral. All our belongings were destroyed.

SF Practitioner. Are the clean clothes part of the 4 too, or is that a higher number? **(SF Scaling Question).**

Peter: The clean clothes are important, even if we just somehow manage to clean up the clothes we are wearing right now, the clothes we have on our backs.

SF Practitioner: Would the clean clothes be part of making it a 5? **(SF Scaling Question).**

Peter: I guess so, actually it would probably even be a 5 or 5 1/2.

SF Practitioner: And what will be the next thing that needs to happen?

Peter: It may actually need to happen even before finding a way to have clean clothes. I need to actually find out whether my family can be buried in our family's cemetery space, or if that is closed off because of the fighting going on near there. If so, I will need to make other arrangements.

SF Practitioner: Finding out where they can be buried.

Peter: (He puts his head in his hands and cries) It is so hard ...

SF Practitioner: Of course. I am sure it is harder that it is possible to say with words. Do you think it might be helpful to talk about what you are feeling right now?[20]

Peter: No, I really need to focus on taking care of my son and arranging for the burials. I need to take care of this. It is my responsibility.

SF Practitioner: You want to carry out your responsibility[21] despite how hard things are right now.

Peter: Yes, it is what I need to do.

SF Practitioner: Where are you finding the strength to go forward with this?[22]

Peter: I love my son and I love my wife and my daughters. They are everything to me.

SF Practitioner: Your love for them is how you are finding the strength?

Peter: Yes.

SF Practitioner: Let's suppose you have managed to make the funeral arrangements and you carry them out ...

Peter: And then the funeral is over.

---

[20]Notice that although the SF practitioner asks if it would be helpful for Peter to talk about his feelings, the direction and content of the session continues to be determined by Peter's goals rather than those of the practitioner.

[21]The SF practitioner is careful to incorporate some of Peter's exact words into the conversation, in this case, *responsibility*. This respectfully demonstrates that the SF practitioner is listening attentively and cares about what Peter is saying.

[22]Asking Peter where he is *finding the strength* is not only an Indirect Compliment. It also serves to implicitly remind Peter of personal strengths which will hopefully help him to navigate through the complex emotions that will likely come up during the process of fulfilling his burial responsibilities and grieving the loss of his wife and children.

SF Practitioner: And then the funeral is over and you know deep inside that you have done the best you possibly could do under the circumstances. What number will that be? **(SF Scaling Question).**

Peter: That will be an 8.

SF Practitioner: What will be happening when it is 10?

Peter: Some time will need to pass. And I must continue to look after my boy, to comfort him and keep him safe, whatever that takes.

SF Practitioner: Whatever that takes.[23]

Peter: Yes.

SF Practitioner: It is obvious to me that you are a very courageous man and that you deeply love your family.[24] **(SF Direct Compliment).**

Peter: I do really love my family but I do not feel courageous right now. I feel that I am just doing what I have to do.

SF Practitioner: For you right now, it is more about the doing.[25]

Peter: Yes. That is true.

SF Practitioner: Is there anything else that I you think I should ask you or that would be important to tell me?[26] **(Safety Net Question).**

Peter: I think not right now. It feels complete as it can be for now.

SF Practitioner: I would be happy to talk with you if you want to meet again. I also want to say that it is clear to me that you are a devoted father and husband.

Peter: Thank you for that. And I will try to come and see you again after the funeral. Thank you.

SF Practitioner: You are welcome. I will be here if you decide it would be helpful to come back.

SESSION ENDS

DISCUSSION

As can be seen in this transcript of Peter's session, SF scaling questions can be an effective way to help people find the strength to

---

[23]Notice how SF practitioners are careful to incorporate the client's exact words whenever helpful.

[24]This is a *Direct Compliment*. SF practitioners try to never miss an opportunity to give a legitimate compliment based on what they observe in a session.

[25]Notice how the SF practitioner is careful to utilise the client's exact words whenever possible.

[26]This is an example of the **Safety Net Question** which SF practitioners ask to ensure that they have not inadvertently missed something important. SF sessions traditionally end after the Safety Net Question has been asked and the client has been given some compliments. In situations like Peter's, it can be particularly important to ask the Safety Net Question in order to give the clients an opportunity to reach out for help in the event that they may be feeling suicidal in response to the recent traumatic event(s) they have endured.

cope with extremely painful situations associated with traumatic events by generating a structure to plan and carry out difficult but necessary responsibilities in the immediate aftermath.

Explaining the reason for drawing the SF scale and respectfully asking permission beforehand is especially important in situations like Peter's because people who have experienced recent trauma very understandably tend to dislike surprises and unpredictability. As demonstrated in the previous case example in this chapter, scaling questions can be extremely helpful for people in the process of navigating the aftermath of traumatic experiences when offered in a sensitive and caring manner and prefaced by a respectful explanation. And perhaps because portions of the brain associated with evaluative thinking are activated in response to these questions, answering scaling questions seems to have a calming effect that counterbalances the intensity of painful emotions.

Although the SF practitioner gently asks Peter if it would be helpful to talk about his feelings, the SF practitioner deliberately does not pressure Peter to do so. Consistent with the SF approach, the SF practitioner recognises that Peter is the best expert on his own life and what he needs at the moment. The fact that the session continues to be determined by Peter's goals illustrates an important difference between SFT and traditional psychotherapy models. In the latter case, it would usually be the professional rather than the client who determines the direction of the session.

The next case excerpt will illustrate how the SFBT approach can be utilised to help trauma survivors cope while navigating ongoing change.

CASE EXAMPLE: OKSAMA – A TRAUMATISED REFUGEE

This session takes place in a community support center that provides counseling and information about available resources for people coping with homelessness. A mother of three young children, Oksama is a war refugee who has recently witnessed repeated bombings and horrific atrocities in her home town. The SF practitioner greets Oksama and welcomes her warmly. They exchange introductions and sit down in the practitioners' office.

SF Practitioner: I am very pleased to meet you.
Oksama: Thank you for seeing me. I have been feeling pretty desperate.

SF Practitioner: I want to do my best to be helpful today in whatever way I can. Is it okay if I ask you a few questions in order to help me best understand what you have been experiencing and how I might be most helpful?[27] **(SF Goal Development Question).**

Oksama: My children and I had to flee our home city two weeks ago because it was no longer safe for us. My husband traveled with us to the train station and waited with us until we were able to get on a train. He could not come with us because he is not allowed to leave the country. At first we were able to communicate with each other on our cell phones, but now I have not heard from him for the past 4 days. I don't know if his phone is no longer charging because there is no electricity in the city after the bombings, or if he maybe lost it, or if something terrible has happened to him ...I don't even know if he is still alive. (She begins sobbing).

SF Practitioner: I am so very sorry. (She offers Oksama a tissue). *I think there are no words that can truly express how frightening this must be for you and your children.*

Oksama: There truly are not. You cannot imagine.

SF Practitioner: I am sure that is true ...

I want to do whatever I can to be helpful today. Our time is unfortunately somewhat limited, so I want to make sure that we[28] *use this hour in whatever way would be most useful for you. What do you think would be most helpful for us to focus on today in order for you to be able to honestly feel afterward that coming here had been helpful?* **(SF Goal Development Question).**

Oksama: I really don't know. (She begins sobbing again and the SF Practitioner hands her a tissue). *It all just feels so unreal. And so scary.*

SF Practitioner: Of course. (There is a teapot sitting on the table between them and the SF practitioner makes a gesture to offer Oksama a cup of tea).

Oksama: (She responds with a nod, accepts a cup of tea and wraps her hands around the warm cup).[29]

Oksama: I don't know what to say. Everything feels impossible.

---

[27]Traumatised clients benefit from being reassured about the SF practitioner's positive intentions and being asked permission prior to asking questions.

[28]Notice how the SF practitioner's use of "we" implies a collaborative relationship.

[29]Not all SF communication is necessarily verbal. Depending on their culture some SF practitioners might convey support and comfort to their clients through simple gestures like as offering a tissue or pouring them a cup of tea.

SF Practitioner: Of course. And I can only imagine that it was not easy for you to get on the train. And yet somehow you did it, you got yourself and your children to safety. That is very impressive.[30] **(SF Direct Compliment).**
Oksama: What choice did I have? (She seems angry).
SF Practitioner: How did you do it? (Her tone is respectful and appreciative. **(Indirect Compliment).**
Oksama: My husband and I had to wait on the platform with our children for a very long time. It was very crowded and we were all out in the cold. In the end we thought we probably would not be able to get onto the train at all because it was already very crowded when it arrived with people already standing in the aisles. But we were desperate.

I was very worried about my youngest who already had a cold. So my husband and and I took a risk and began quickly passing our children up to the train window where a kind old man pulled them onto the train. Then I ran to the train door which was already closing and began screaming as loud as I could, 'You have to let me on, my little children are on this train.' The conductor opened the door and very quickly pulled me on the train. I looked out and say my husband looking at me with a smile on his face and holding one of his thumbs up as if to say, You did it. That was the last time I saw my husband. I hope I see him again. (Her voice is flat and she sounds worried).
SF Practitioner: I hope so, too. What an experience you and your family have gone through! How did you and your husband find the strength and courage to get your children on that train? **(SF Indirect Compliment).**[31]
Oksama: We are the kind of parents who refuse to give up. We would do absolutely anything for our children, even if it means making other people angry. Our children are everything to us. They are our life. We would always do everything necessary to keep them safe, whatever it takes.
SF Practitioner: You are the kind of parents who would definitely do that.[32] **(SF Direct Compliment).**
Oksama: Yes.
SF Practitioner: How old are your children?
Oksama: My son is 9, and my three little girls are 6,5, and 2 1/2.

---

[30]This is a direct compliment. While some clients feel supported by direct compliments, not everyone responds well to them, particularly in crisis situations. When this evident the SF practitioner immediately shifts to SF Indirect Compliments.

[31]*Indirect Compliments* in the form of asking "how did you do it" serve to elicit a self-compliment from the client.

[32]Although Oksama rejected an earlier Direct Compliment, she seems to feel comfortable accepting this one. This perhaps suggests that she is feeling somewhat more comfortable with the SF practitioner.

SF Practitioner: What are their names?

Oksama: My son is Dmytro, after his father. The girls are Nattallya, Kateryna, and Sofia. Nattallya was named after my late mother.

SF Practitioner: Where are they right now?

Oksama: They are in the waiting room playing with toys. One of the other women from the shelter came with me to watch them while we met.

SF Practitioner: I would like to meet them when we are finished if there is time.[33]

Oksama: Okay.

SF Practitioner: May I ask you another question?

Oksama: All right. (She seems slightly more relaxed).

SF Practitioner: What needs to happen as a result of our meeting in order for you and your children to know afterwards that it had been a good idea for you to come here? **(SF Goal Development Question).**[34]

Oksama: I don't know ... .

SF Practitioner: *(Nods encouragingly).*[35]

Oksama: The thing is I don't know what we will do when we have to leave the shelter. I have no plan. And I don't know how I will find my husband, how I will let him know where we are.

SF Practitioner: *You need to have a plan for when you leave the shelter and also a plan for how you will let your husband know where you are? Would it be helpful to focus on plans today?*

Oksama: *Yes. The first thing is finding a place for us to stay when we leave the shelter. But I don't know where to begin. I also need to figure out a plan for how to let my husband know where we are ...*

SF Practitioner: That makes sense. These seem like good goals. (Oksama nods).

There is a simple technique called scaling that is helpful when people need to figure out clear plans in situations like this. It involves my drawing a little line on a piece of paper. Is it ok if I draw this?'[36]

Oksama: OK.

The SF practitioner takes out a piece of paper and draws a line.

---

[33]The SF practitioner's gesture of expressing a desire to meet the children serves to communicate respect and convey appreciation of the fact that Oksama's children are extremely important to her.

[34]Because Oksama has not yet described a goal, the SF practitioner gently repeats the question.

[35]Notice that the SF practitioner does not speak but simply nods encouragingly and waits for Oksama answer. Oftentimes, clients who have experienced recent trauma need a moment of two of silence in order to formulate their thoughts. Because goals are essential to the solution-development process, SF practitioners typically continue to politely ask **Goal Development Questions** until the client manages to identify a goal.

[36]Notice how the SF practitioner asks permission before proceeding.

Let's suppose that 0 represents before you started thinking about the need for a plan for when you leave the shelter and a plan for how to let your husband know where you and your children are staying and 10 represents when you have already carried out the plan,

0———————————————————————————————————————10

We know you are not at 0 because the represented before you started thinking about the need for a plan and we know you are not at 10 yet because you haven't carried out the plan yet.

Can you make mark on the line to show where you are now? (She hands Oksama the paper and a pencil) (**SF Scaling Question**).

Oksama: (She sits silently for a few seconds and then draws a mark approximately at the 1 point).

SF Practitioner: What number should we call that? (**SF Scaling Question**).

Oksama: It is a 1 because at least I know I need to make a plan. But I don't have any idea how to move forward. The whole situation feels impossible.

SF Practitioner: That is what this scale is for. It will help us[37] figure that out.

Oksama: Ok. (She seems slightly less anxious).

SF Practitioner: Is it okay if I ask you another question? This is kind of a strange question, but it will help us both begin to get a clearer picture of what needs to happen next. It requires some some imagination and some mental effort. Are you willing to give it a try?

Oksama: Yes, of course. I will do anything to try to help my family.

SF Practitioner: Let's suppose that tonight you and your children go back to the shelter and eventually it becomes late and you all go to sleep. Sometime during the night however something special happens. But you don't know this because you are sleeping. What happens is a sort of miracle in that when you wake up in the morning you are suddenly at a 2. What would you notice first that is different that would tell you that something has changed and that you are now at a 2 and not at a 1? (**SF Miracle Question**).

Oksama: The first thing that comes to my mind is that I would know where I can go to leave a message for my husband and would know who to talk to about finding a place to stay when we have to leave the shelter – I don't know how long we are allowed to stay at the shelter.

---

[37]Notice how the SF practitioner uses *us* to convey that this will be a collaborative process. Oksama will be neither left to her own devices in formulating this nor will she be put in a "one-down" position by the practitioner simply telling her what to do. This detail illustrates one of the ways that SFT functions to empower trauma survivors.

SF Practitioner: Knowing where to the leave the message, finding out how long you can stay at this shelter, and who you can talk to about finding a place to go next?

Oksama: Yes. And how I will feed my children.

SF Practitioner: Of course, and how you will feed your children. Let's start with the message you want to leave for your husband. Right now the Red Cross has contact points in most of the large cities in your country where you can leave messages for loved ones. I will make sure that our receptionist gives you the Red Cross refugee contact number as soon as we are done with this session. It is posted on the wall behind the reception desk.[38] So let's suppose that you now know where to leave the message, what number will you be on the scale? **(SF Scaling Question).**

Oksama: Probably a 3. If I heard from my husband, I would be a 10 because then we could make a plan together.

SF Practitioner: Of course. That makes perfect sense. Regarding getting in touch with your husband, in addition to the Red Cross contact number we will of course give you, is there anything else that would be helpful for getting in contact with perhaps someone else who might be likely to see him and might be able to get a message to him?

Oksama: Maybe his uncle. His uncle is crippled and too old to be required to join the army, so he is probably still in the shelter in his home village unless something has happened to him.

SF Practitioner: Let's suppose you get a message to his uncle, will that raise the number on the scale? **(SF Scaling Question).**

Oksama: Yes, a little bit. That would make it a 1 and 1/2, I suppose.

SF Practitioner: Would it be helpful to also leave a message for your husband at your country's embassy in Poland?

Oksama: I think that would be a good idea.

SF Practitioner: Let's suppose you do that, what number would that make it on the scale? **(SF Scaling Question).**

Oksama: Still about a 1 1/2.

SF Practitioner: Would it be helpful if I gave you the number and email for your country's embassy here? [39]

Oksama: Yes. Could you do that?

SF Practitioner: Yes, and if you like you could leave a message right now. You could do it either by phone or email.

---

[38]Notice that the SF practitioner does not hesitate to respectfully address the client's need for the phone number before continuing the solution-development process.

[39]Although the SFBT approach emphasises utilising clients' already existing resources, SF practitioners do not hesitate to offer important information that they think the client might need or find helpful in order to move forward.

Oksama: I think the phone is better because my writing is not so good in a foreign language.

SF Practitioner: Shall we call the embassy right now?

Oksama: Yes. That would be great.

SF Practitioner: (Types a phone number into an iPhone and then hands it to Oksama).

Oksama: I am here with my children and I want to leave a message through the embassy for my husband in case he is trying to find us. (She then gives her name, the children's name, the name of the shelter where they are staying, and the number of her personal cell phone and hangs up the phone after a few minutes).

SF Practitioner: Was that helpful? (Oksama nods). What number are you on the scale now that you have left the message? **(SF Scaling Question).**

Oksama: I think I have moved to a 2 now.[40] They also said I might try calling the Red Cross in case they have some information on my husband. I am also going to try calling his Uncle later today on the old number I have.

SF Practitioner: What else will help you move forward on the scale? **(SF Scaling Question).**

Oksama: I need to talk to someone about what we will do, where we will stay and if we cannot return to our country, where we could go if we are are told we have to leave the shelter where we are currently staying.

SF Practitioner: I am familiar with your shelter's policies because I volunteer there part-time. They are definitely not going to turn you out until you have found another place to stay. Have you heard anything about additional places that people can stay?

Oksama: That is really good to know. I heard that some of the churches and synagogues are helping people find more permanent places to stay.

SF Practitioner: Do you have a list of the names?

Oksama: No, I just heard about it from another woman staying at the shelter.

SF Practitioner: I am happy to give you a printed list of the names, addresses, and phone numbers of the organisations that are helping people find permanent places to stay.

Oksama: Thank you.

SF Practitioner: Is there anything else I should ask you about or that it would be helpful for us to talk about? **(SF Safety Net Question).**

Oksama: I can't sleep at night and my kids are having trouble too. I wonder if you could give me some pills.

SF Practitioner: I am unable to provide any pills, but I will give you a medical referral to see someone who might be able to help with that. Meanwhile, I

---

[40]It is not unusual for clients to go up on the scale during a session.

wonder if there is anything at all that you have found so far that is helpful in getting you relaxed enough to sleep. **(SF Exception Question).**

Oksama: It seems to help them if we sing a little song together when they are in bed. We have to do it softly because of the other people, but it seems to help calm them done.

SF Practitioner: Maybe hearing the song helps some of the other people too?

Oksama: Maybe.

SF Practitioner: You have discovered that singing is sometimes helpful. I wonder if you are perhaps also doing some other things that are sometimes helpful, even a little bit? **(SF What Else Question).**

Oksama: Sometimes I just lay under the covers and pray.

SF Practitioner: Is that helpful as well? **(SF Exception Question).**

Oksama: Yes, I think it is. After I pray I feel calmer and a little bit more hopeful.

SF Practitioner: Where did you learn to do that? **(SF Indirect Compliment).**

Oksama: My mother and my grandmother. My father was not a believer, but my mother and both my grandmothers were. They are both gone now.

SF Practitioner: But you still think of them and in that sense they are with you?

Oksama: Yes, of course.

SF Practitioner: I wonder what they would tell you if they were here?[41] **(SF Detail Question).**

Oksama: They would say that they know I am doing the best I can. They would say that they love me.

SF Practitioner: And thinking about them helps? **(SF Exception Question).**

Oksama: A little bit.

SF Practitioner: I would like to invite you to come back and see me in a few days. You can make an appointment on the way out if you like. Meanwhile, I would like to invite you to pay attention to anything you or anyone else does or says, or anything that you learn that helps you move up on your scale even a little bit.

  Would you be willing to do that?

Oksama: Yes, I will.

SF Practitioner: If it is okay, I would like to walk out to the reception area with you and meet your kids, and I will also get you the list of the names of the churches and synagogue here that are helping people and a referral for you to see the nurse.

Oksama: I would like that. You can meet my friend, too. Thank you for talking to me.

SF Practitioner: I look forward to us meeting again. (She hands Oksama the paper with the scale on it).

---

[41]SF practitioners recognise that asking details about a resource, in this case the memory of a supportive loved one, can serve to further strengthen the positive effect.

SESSION ENDS

DISCUSSION

Early on in the session, the SF practitioner's use of the word *we* sets the tone for a collaborative relationship with Oksama. In addition to an overall attentiveness to language, SF practitioners also sometimes utilise non-verbal gestures such as offering their clients a tissue or a cup of tea to gently convey a sense of safety and comfort as happened in this session.

The SF practitioner deliberately uses words like *we* and *us* to send the implicit message that the session is going to be a collaborative process in which Oksama will neither be abandoned solely to her own devices nor will put in a "one-down" position by the practitioner simply telling her what to do.

Although the setting is a community center designed to provide practical information and immediate assistance as well as counseling, the SF practitioner manages to maintain a collaborative solution-focused stance while also addressing the client's need to get in touch with her husband, the ongoing need to find a place to stay for herself and her children, and her wish to formulate future plans.

CHAPTER SUMMARY

SFT is a trauma-informed therapy that has been applied to treating Post-Traumatic Stress Disorder is a variety of contexts, including natural disasters, domestic violence, rape, sexual or physical assault, bullying, or war combat experiences.

SFT practitioners apply the SF approach to help people resolve the effects of painful life experiences associated with PTSD by utilising clients' existing resources and strengths to create a satisfying and rewarding future that counterbalances and displaces post-traumatic symptoms. As evidenced by this chapter's final case example, the SF approach can also be applied in situations that require practitioners to provide information about additional resources such as housing, refugee services, and other services.

Experiential Exercise: Coping with a Challenging Experience

Think of a time in the past when you successfully coped with a stressful or challenging experience. What helped you cope? What personal qualities or strengths did you utilise in order to cope? How did you develop those strengths? Is there anything else that you did or someone else did that helped you to cope? What did you learn from this experience?

Now think of something in your current life that you find challenging? What has proven helpful so far in helping you cope with this situation? What else? On a scale of 0–10 in which 10 represents Optimal Coping and 0 represents the Opposite, where are you now? What makes it that number? What would it look like if you suddenly found that you were a point higher? Experiment with paying attention to anything that you or others do that helps you move up or maintain your current position on your Coping Scale.

REFERENCES

Althobaiti, S., Kazantzis, N., Ofori-Asenso, R., Romero, L., Fisher, J., Mills, K. E., & Liew, D. (2020). Efficacy of interpersonal psychotherapy for post-traumatic stress disorder: A systematic review and meta-analysis. *Journal of Affective Disorders, 264*, 286–294.

Bannick, R. (2014). *Post-traumatic success.* New York: W.W. Norton.

de Shazer, S., Dolan, Y., Korman, H., McCollum, E., Trepper, T., & Berg, I. K. (2021). *More than miracles: The state of the art of Solution-focused Brief Therapy, 2nd Ed.* London: Routledge Press.

Dolan, Y. (1991). *Resolving sexual abuse: Solution-focused therapy and Ericksonian hypnosis for adult survivors.* New York: W.W. Norton.

Dolan, Y. (2000). *One small step: Moving beyond trauma and therapy to a life of joy.* Bloomington, Indiana: iUniverse.

Dolan, Y. (2006). Personal conversation with Insoo Kim Berg.

Eads, R., & Lee, M. Y. (2019). Solution-Focused Therapy for trauma survivors: A review of the outcome literature. *Journal of Solution-Focused Practices, 3*(1), 9.

Hendon, J. (2011). *Beating combat stress: 101 techniques for recovery.* New York: Wiley.

Hendon, J. (2017). *What it takes to thrive: Techniques for severe trauma and stress recovery.* Hackensack, NJ: World Scientific Publishing Company Pte Ltd.

Kim, J. S. (2018). Intersection of SFBT and Trauma. In A. S. Froerer, J. von Cziffra-Bergs, J. Kim, & E. Connie (Eds.), *Solution-focused brief therapy with clients managing trauma.* Oxford University Press, pp. 10–24.

Kim, J. S., Brook, J., & Akin, B. (2021). Randomized controlled trial of solution-focused brief therapy for substance-use-disorder-affected parents involved in the child welfare system. *Journal of the Society for Social Work and Research, 12*(3), 545–568.

Kim, J. S., and Froerer, A. S. (2018). Intersection of SFBT and trauma. In A. S. Froerer, J. von Cziffra-Bergs, J. Kim, and E. Connie (Eds.), *Solution-focused brief therapy with clients managing trauma.* New York: Oxford Press.

Kim, J., Jordan, S. S., Franklin, C., & Froerer, A. (2019). Is solution-focused brief therapy evidence-based? An update 10 years later. *Families in Society, 100*(2), 127–138.

National Institute of Mental Health (2023, May 22). *Post-traumatic stress disorder.* Retrieved from https://www.nimh.nih.gov/health/statistics/post-traumatic-stress-disorder-ptsd.

Polusny, M. A., Erbes, C. R., Thuras, P., Moran, A., Lamberty, G. J., Collins, R. C., ... & Lim, K. O. (2015). Mindfulness-based stress reduction for posttraumatic stress disorder among veterans: A randomized clinical trial. *JAMA, 314*(5), 456–465.

Rand, K. L., & Cheavens, J. S. (2009). Hope theory. *Oxford Handbook of Positive Psychology, 2*, 323–333.

Roberts, N. P., Roberts, P. A., Jones, N., & Bisson, J. I. (2015). Psychological interventions for post-traumatic stress disorder and comorbid substance use disorder: A systematic review and meta-analysis. *Clinical Psychology Review, 38*, 25–38.

von Cziffra-Bergs, J. (2018). SFBT and violent crime. In A. S.-B. Froerer (Ed.), *Solution-focused brief therapy with clients managing trauma.* New York: Oxford Press, pp. 57–58.

SOLUTION-FOCUSED COACHING IN BUSINESS SETTINGS

As with other SF practices, which have been found to work as well or better than problem-focused approaches, Solution-Focused Counseling (SFC) has been shown to be highly effective for business coaching (Grant, 2012; Grant & Gerrard, 2020; Theeboom et al., 2016). This chapter demonstrates some of the ways that SF Business Coaches utilise the SF approach in their everyday work. Illustrative transcripts demonstrate what SFC looks like when an SF coach works with a newly unemployed executive seeking to restart his career, and a disgruntled employee whose boss orders her to see a business coach.

At its core, SFC closely resembles SFT (Iveson et al., 2012, p. 5; Szabo & Meier, 2009). Both SFT and SFC are future-focused and goal-driven, emphasise resources, and view clients as the primary experts on their own lives. Further, they are characterised by a similar solution-development process in which **SF What Else Questions** and **Direct and/or Indirect SF Compliments** are utilised to highlight the client's strengths whenever applicable, and scales are utilised to assess and formulate further progress toward goals.

Here is a quick overview of the SFC process:

1. SF coaches and their clients work collaboratively to generate a detailed description of how the client's life will be different once their goal, or "best hope," has been achieved.
2. Once a goal has been identified, SF coaches and their clients explore the clients' already existing behaviors and strengths in order to find the resources needed to achieve the goal.
3. The SF coach introduces a 0–10 SF Scale in which 10 represents a point at which the client has fully achieved the Goal and 0 represents the Opposite.

DOI: 10.4324/9781003401230-6

4. The clients rate their current position on the scale and describe the details associated with moving in the direction of the 10, e.g. "What would you find yourself doing differently if you found that you were 1 point higher" or "what might your co-workers notice you doing if you were a point higher?"
5. The SF coach and client discuss the client's current progress toward the goal and identify future behaviors that will either demonstrate further progress or serve to maintain current progress. They also address additional goals as needed.

As reflected in the five steps listed previously, the SFC process is remarkably similar to applications of the approach with other client populations; it is the scope and context of the goal that primarily distinguishes SFC from SFT. In contrast to SFT, which typically focuses on clients' personal or family life, or SF in school settings, which address educational goals, SFC sessions primarily focus on the client's work life, e.g. their professional aspirations and relationships with co-workers, bosses, supervisors, or supervises. And in addition to people seeking help with professional goals, SFC session are sometimes instigated by a supervisor or boss in an effort to retain an employee.

Thanks to the elasticity of the SF approach, SF coaches are able to accommodate a wide range of employee, supervisory, and executive contexts, challenges and goals. For example, the same SF question, "What is your best hope for your organization?" (Hogan, D., 2017, p. 252) can be utilised to generate productive information from people working in a wide spectrum of positions ranging from entry-level employees to supervisors, quality assurance evaluators to corporate executives.

Let's begin our exploration of SFC with the following session involving a recently unemployed business executive trying to restart his career.

SOLUTION-FOCUSED COACHING WITH AN UNEMPLOYED EXECUTIVE: *I NEED TO GET MY CONFIDENCE BACK*

John, age 43, had recently lost his management job following the sale of the mid-sized paint company where he had worked for the past 15 years. Despite having been a highly productive and loyal employee, he was given minimal notice of the termination of his position and no acknowledgment of the significant contributions he had made to the company's success. And John's dismissal had come at a particularly difficult time. His wife had recently been diagnosed with a terminal illness and his daughter was enrolled at an expensive private college.

> *SF Coach:* (After exchanging mutual introductions and pleasantries). *What is your best hope regarding how this session could prove useful?* (**SF Goal Development Question**).
>
> *John:* I would feel that I had gotten some of my confidence back.
>
> *SF Coach: Getting your confidence back? You're accustomed[1] to having more confidence?*
>
> *John:* Oh yes. I used to feel very confident in my work before my company was sold and my position was terminated.
>
> *SF Coach: The fact that you were confident in your work suggests that there are things that you are good at in your work.[2] What are some of the parts of your work that you are good at?*
>
> *John:* I am – at least I used to be – very good at sales. I was good at listening to the customer and matching our products with what they needed.
>
> *SF Coach: Those are two very important aspects of sales.* (**SF Direct Compliment**).
>
> How did you become good at these things – listening to customers and matching products to their needs? (**SF Indirect Compliment**).
>
> *John:* I spent a lot of time familiarising myself with the product, and I attended some university classes on communication skills.
>
> *SF Coach: You are clearly someone who is willing to do what it takes to be good at your job.* (**SF Direct Compliment**).
>
> *John:* Thanks. I guess I've never been afraid of going the extra mile.
>
> *SF Coach: That is clearly true. What else are you good at[3] in your work?* (**SF What Else Question**).

---

[1] The coach's wording, "You are accustomed to having more confidence," typifies SF practitioners' careful attention to language. "Accustomed to" emphasises that the client is still capable of confidence while "you used to have confidence" implies its loss.

[2] Notice how quickly the SF coach identifies a potential indication of the client's strength.

[3] This is another version of the **SF What Else Question.** Repeatedly asking "what else are you good at" in your work is a SF technique created and popularised by the founders of BRIEF, an independent training and consultation agency in the practice of SFT in London. In reference to John's case, it also serves to generate a description of various previous experiences of confidence.

John: I was ... am good at keeping careful records of customer's sales histories, documenting their pattern of purchasing our products record keeping, and documenting product purchase patterns. I never missed a deadline. And I always managed to fulfill the target levels suggested by my bosses.

SF Coach: Wow. **(SF Direct Compliment)**. And what do you think your former bosses might say you are good at?

John: I don't know ... I guess they would say that I was a loyal employee who got along well with co-workers and people working at all levels of our organisation.

SF Coach: What do you think it was that allowed you to do that so well? **(SF Indirect Compliment)**.

John: I always try to give people the benefit of the doubt, and the result is I very seldom get into a conflict with anyone.

SF Coach: That is another significant strength. **(SF Direct Compliment)**. Not that there should be – this is already a lot – but is there anything else that you are good at in your work? **(SF What Else Question)**.

John: I can't think of anything.

SF Coach: I don't want to lose track of your goal of feeling confident again. Is it okay if I ask you a Scaling Question? (John nods). Suppose that there is a 0–10 scale in which 10 represents your having the highest, most optimal level of confidence, and 0 represents the Opposite. Where would you say you are right now on that scale? **(SF Scaling Question)**.

John: (After pausing for a few seconds) I guess I would say that I am at a 4.

SF Coach: What contributes to it being a 4 and not a lower number? **(SF Scaling Question)**.

John: Actually if you had asked me to rate my confidence level when I first walked into this office, I think it would probably have been lower. Talking about the things that I am good at in my work probably raised it a little.

SF Coach: What else contributes to it being a 4? **(SF What Else Question)**.

John: The fact that I have had 20 years of work experience and also that I am very motivated. I need to earn a living in order to support my wife and pay for my daughter's college expenses.

SF Coach: You have had a lot of experience and you are clearly motivated. **(SF Direct Compliment)**.

John: I really am.

SF Coach: Let's suppose that you suddenly found yourself at a 10 on your Confidence Scale and your confidence is clearly back. What would be the first difference that you or someone else would notice? **(SF Scaling Question)**.

John: My wife would notice that my sense of humor was back and I would start sending in job applications.

SF Coach: Let's suppose your sense of humor has returned and you find yourself sending in job applications, what happens next now that your confidence is back?

John: Hopefully, I would get some job interviews. That is both what I want and what I am currently most afraid of ...[4]

SF Coach: So how would the fact that your confidence is back up[5] when you are invited to job interviews affect you? What is the first thing that you would notice?

John: The first thing I would probably notice is that I would be sleeping okay. I might think about the upcoming interview, but I wouldn't obsess about it and start laying awake all night worrying about it.

SF Coach: You would be sleeping ok. (John nods). What else? **(SF What Else Question).**

John: I wouldn't be nervous on the morning of the job interview.

SF Coach: How would you being feeling instead on the morning of the job interview? **(SF Detail Question).**

John: I would get up on the morning of the job interview and I would be in a good mood. I wouldn't be nervous[6] – I would be feeling confident, even a bit optimistic.

SF Coach: What would your wife and daughter see you doing that day that would likely give then the idea that you are in a good mood and that you are feeling confident and a bit optimistic? **(SF Detail Question).**

John: They would see me getting up early and making coffee. I might even make a quick run to the store and come home with fresh bagels for breakfast. And I would take the dog with me in the car on the way to the bagel shop. He loves car rides. Those are things that I used to do regularly before I lost my job.

SF Coach: Let's suppose you do something like that, how will they likely react?

John: Oh, my wife and daughter would definitely like it. And the dog would definitely like the car ride. (He smiles).

SF Coach: How else will your confidence show up on the interview day? **(SF Detail Question).**

John: I would be more talkative. I might make a joke about something that happened that morning or even later in the day while I was in the process of the waiting for the interview.

SF Coach: Your sense of humor will clearly be back. (Client nods in agreement.) What else will be different that would indicate that your confidence is back?

---

[4]At this point, the SF coach could ask "What would you want to be experiencing instead of fear," but since this outcome has already been implied by the client's goal of feeling confident, it is more productive to ask how behaviors associated with John's confidence show up when he is invited to come for an interview.

[5]Notice the SF coach's careful attending to language here. The word *next* in the previous question further emphasises that John's confidence is now back in accordance with his goal.

[6]This is another instance when the SF coach could have asked an **SF Instead Question**, but does not do so because it is unnecessary. The client has already identified the instead by saying that he would be in a good mood.

John: I would start asking former colleagues, supervisors, and bosses for permission to list their names as references on my job application.

SF Coach: What else goes with that 10 on your confidence scale?

John: Well, the ultimate thing will be that I will have a job and it will be a job that I feel good about.

SF Coach: What will contribute to you feeling good about your job?

John: The salary will be commensurate with my experience and skills.

SF Coach: Commensurate with your experience and skills.[7]

John: I would be confident that is what I deserved and it would show in the way I conducted myself during the interview.

SF Coach: What will that look like? **(SF Detail Question).**

John: It's hard to say, but I know what it will look like because I used to be like that. I guess my body language will reflect a sort of relaxed but attentive, confident position. Not too casual and not too formal. It would probably show up in the way I walked into the interview room, how I sat down, how I responded to the interview questions.

SF Coach: And you know what that means for you because you have experienced it before.

John: Exactly.

SF Coach: I think that you have done a very good job of describing what having your confidence back will look like. **(SF Direct Compliment).** Is there anything else that I should ask before our time is up today? **(SF Safety Net Question).**

John: No, I think this covers it.

SF Coach: In that case, I would simply encourage you to continue to pay attention to anything you do or anyone else does that contributes to you moving higher up your confidence scale or helps you maintain your current level at the moment.

John: Okay. I can do that. I am already feeling somewhat better.

SF Coach: I am glad to hear that. I has been a pleasure to work with you today. Please feel free to contact me if you decide you would like a follow-up session.

John: I definitely will. Thanks.

SF Coach: You are very welcome.

SESSION ENDS.

Follow-Up

John did not schedule further sessions, however two weeks later he emailed the SF coach to report that he had scheduled three job interviews. Six weeks later he wrote again to report that he had

---

[7]Notice how the SF coach utilises the client's exact words.

found a job that he liked and was now at an 8 on the Confidence Scale. And a few months later, he referred a colleague for coaching.

DISCUSSION

The session begins with the SF Coach asking "What is your best hope for how this session could prove useful?" Following that, the most significant feature of this coaching session is what the coach does NOT do. While it might seem obvious for to directly ask John what he will need to do or what it will "take" in to regain his confidence, those sorts of questions might contribute further to his current state of stress. But asking questions about what it would be like for John to simply "find" himself in a more desirable position allows him to immediately start identifying the behaviors associated with that state, thereby making it more realistically approachable. Effect is similar to asking the SF Miracle question described in earlier chapters; it specifically spotlights behaviors associated with John's goal, for example feeling more confident about work.

Similarly, when John expresses that being invited for a job interview is something that could cause him to lay awake at night obsessing, the SF coach continues to pursue the already stipulated goal (feeling confident) by asking how John's confidence will show up prior to and during the job interviews.

While it might have seemed intuitive to ask an **SF Instead Question**, for example "What would you like to be experiencing instead of obsessing or having trouble sleeping," focusing on how the confidence would evidence itself the night before and during the job interview approaches the goal in a more efficient way. It also remains consistent with the goal-directed nature of the SF approach.

A further example of the careful word choices that characterise the SF approach is the coach's statement that "You are accustomed to having more confidence." This statement implies that John remains capable of confidence, as opposed to saying "You used to have confidence," which would suggest the opposite.

By repeatedly asking John "What else are you good at in your work" (Ratner et al., 2012), the SF coach elicits numerous additional reasons to feel confident and examples of times when he has felt more confident. Generating numerous examples of SF Exceptions or resources prior to introducing the SF Scale further supports the goal of restoring John's confidence.

The session ends with the SF coach encouraging John to pay attention to anything that helps him progress in the direction of the 10 or to maintain his current progress. Unlike suggesting behavioral steps (submitting job applications, contacting potential references) which could further deplete Johns' confidence if he failed to accomplish them, simply inviting John to notice what he does to make things better or maintain his progress provides the sufficient elasticity to accommodate his real-life capabilities and personal time frame.

SOLUTION-FOCUSED COACHING WITH A DISGRUNTLED EMPLOYEE: *I'M JUST TRYING TO KEEP MY JOB*

Session 1

SF Coach: I am happy to meet you.

Cassandra: I wish I could say the same. The only reason I am here is because my supervisor is requiring me to see you.

SF Coach: What would need to happen as a result of coming here in order for it to have useful and for you to be able to say afterward that it had not been a waste of your time? (**SF Goal Development Question**).

Cassandra: The only thing I can think of is that I wouldn't need to come back. I don't want to be here. I am only here because my supervisor is requiring me to come and I don't want to lose my job.

SF Coach: Of course. You are here because you want to keep your job. Is that what we should focus on today? (**SF Goal Development Question**).

Cassandra: I don't really care what we focus on. I just want to get my supervisor off my back so I don't keep getting deficiency notices and so I don't have to come here anymore.

SF Coach: It sounds like this is a difficult situation.

Cassandra: It IS.

SF Coach: I can appreciate that, and I don't want to waste your time.[8]

Cassandra: And I appreciate that you don't want to waste my time. (Her tone is sarcastic).

SF Coach: Since you are being required to come here, what would be the most useful thing for us to focus on in order for it to truly not have been a waste of your time? (**SF Goal Development Question**).

---

[8]Notice how the SF coach communicates acceptance and positive intent toward the client.

Cassandra: I need this job. I need to keep it.

SF Coach: You need to keep our job, you want to stop getting deficiency notices, and you do not want to have to come here anymore.

Cassandra: Right.

SF Coach: Is the main thing keeping your job? **(SF Goal Development Question).**

Cassandra: Exactly. Like I told you, it's the only reason I am here.

SF Coach: What would your supervisor say needs to be different afterwards in order to be satisfied so that you would not to need to come back?

Cassandra: I don't know. It's hard to say. (After a pause). I guess I would be getting along better with my co-workers. Other than that I think she would have to admit that I am pretty good at my job.

SF Coach: You and she would both agree that you are good at your job?

Cassandra: Yes.

SF Coach: What are some of the things that you are good at in your job?

Cassandra: I am good at solving technical problems with the computerised ordering system.

SF Coach: That sounds like a very important ability. I would imagine that keeping an ordering system working would be crucial for a business. **(SF Indirect Compliment).**

Cassandra: It is.

SF Coach: What else are you good at in your job? **(SF What Else Question).**

Cassandra: I am good at keeping tabs on the individual accounts that make up the larger ones and making sure that we are maintaining the same level of quality on all accounts. We have over 7000 accounts, so it's a lot to keep track of.

SF Coach: Keeping track of that many accounts sounds like an enormous responsibility. **(SF Direct Compliment).** How do you do it? **(SF Indirect Compliment).**

Cassandra: I set up an automated computerised monitoring system that immediately sends out a notice when inventory reaches a critical level.

SF Coach: I can imagine that system is very important for keeping things running smoothly at your company.

Cassandra: It is. I think that is why they haven't fired me.

SF Coach: It sounds like you provide some very valuable things.

Cassandra: I do.

SF Coach: What else are you good at in your job? **(SF What Else Question).**

Cassandra: My co-workers would probably say that I respond very quickly when they need something from me or when they need me to fix some part of the system that is not working well.

SF Coach: What else are you good at in your job?

Cassandra: I am good at keeping track of all the little details that make a difference in whether the system functions the way it's supposed to.

SF Coach: It sounds like all these parts of your work are already going well? (Client nods). I can certainly see why you would be a valued employee. **(Direct SF Compliment).**

Cassandra: I used to think they valued me. But I just got passed over for a yearly promotion and now I am in danger of losing my job.

SF Coach: And as you said earlier,[9] you are here because you want to keep your job?

Cassandra: Yes. As I said before – that is the ONLY reason I am here.

SF Coach: Is it okay if I ask you another question in order to better understand what might be helpful in that direction?[10]

Cassandra: Okay, I guess so.

SF Coach: Let's suppose there is a 0–10 scale where 10 represents that you are completely confident about keeping your job and 0 means the exact opposite. Where would you rate yourself on that scale at the moment? **(SF Scaling Question).**

Cassandra: I guess I would have to think about this for a moment. I am used to medical scales where the higher number means a lot of pain and the lower one means less pain.

SF Coach: That's right. In this kind of scale, the 10 reflects the preferred state – in this case feeling completely comfortable about keeping your job – and 0 means the opposite.

Where would you put yourself on that scale at the moment? **(SF Scaling Question).**

Cassandra: (She pauses for several seconds before answering). I would say that at the moment I am at a 2 ½.

SF Coach: What contributes to your rating it at a 2 ½ and not lower? **(SF Scaling Question).**

Cassandra: I think I would be difficult to easily replace. I have skills that are necessary to the functioning of the business. If I left it might initially take two people to replace me if they were not already up to speed on the technology involved.

SF Coach: What else contributes to the 2 ½? **(SF Scaling Question).**

Cassandra: I have a long history with this company. Next April, I will have been there for 20 years. I had a great working relationship with the original owner who was also my previous boss. But two years ago he retired and turned the company over to his son who was fresh out of an MBA program and thinks he knows everything. Since then everything has been restructured

---

[9] SF coaches, like all competent SF practitioners, are careful to formulate their responses in a way that clearly communicates that they have been listening attentively to everything that the client has previously said.

[10] Notice how the SF coach precedes asking the scaling question by explaining its purpose. This helps to ensure that the client understand that the intent behind the question is positive and not adversarial.

and there is now an office manager and an EAP Dept. (Employee Assistance Program) between me and the boss and I also have an immediate supervisor that I need to report to on a weekly basis. I rarely even see the new boss except of course for last week when he asked to see me because of the so-called deficiency notices I have been receiving from my immediate supervisor.
SF Coach: *So your long history of working there further contributes to the 2 ½. Is there anything else that goes with the 2 ½.*[11] **(SF Scaling Question).**
Cassandra: *Probably the fact that I never take sick days. I am always there and they can always count on me. I even sometimes take extra shifts to fill in for other employees during the holidays because I don't have any living family to get together with on Christmas or Hanukkah.*
SF Coach: *You are someone they can really count on to be there and you are even willing to fill in for other people if needed?*
Cassandra: *Exactly. And that is why I feel so upset about being given these deficiency letters.*
SF Coach: *Understandably. Let's suppose you were no longer receiving deficiency letters. What number would that put you on the scale?* **(SF Scaling Question).**
Cassandra: *It would make a huge difference – that is the thing that I am most upset about. If I weren't getting those letters from my supervisor. I think it would put me at a 7 or an 8, maybe even higher.*
SF Coach: *I realise that a 7 or 8 obviously is not the same as a 10, but do you think that a confidence number like a 7 or an 8 would be a high enough number*[12] *for you to feel reasonably safe about keeping your job?* **(SF Scaling Question).**
Cassandra: *It would not be exactly ideal but it would probably be good enough.*
SF Coach: *So let's suppose that you were at a 7 or 8 and you were no longer receiving deficiency notices from your supervisor and you were no longer being required to come here for coaching session, what would be happening instead?* **(SF Instead Question).**
Cassandra: *I would be getting along better with some of the co-workers who came into my office and asked me for things.*
SF Coach: *What would that look like?* **(SF Detail Question).**
Cassandra: *Well, ideally they wouldn't be bothering me with last minute things. They would plan ahead and give me some time to respond to what they needed.*

---

[11]Notice how in contrast to a problem-focused approach, the SF coach manages to stay focused on the meaning of the 2 ½ rather than exploring the likely "cause" behind the deficiency notices. This reflects the SF tenet that the "cause" is not necessarily related to the solution.
[12]Asking about a potentially "high enough" number on the scale that might be less than a 10 serves to reduce the client's current distance from the goal.

SF Coach: I see. How likely do think it is that they are going to be willing to change in that direction?[13]

Cassandra: Not very likely. They are young and inexperienced and seem to be incapable of planning ahead. This is a very different generation from the one I grew up in.

SF Coach: I can imagine it must not be easy for you when they come in and suddenly need something at the last minute.

Cassandra: It isn't. And they always want it done yesterday. There have been a few times when I have given them a piece of my mind and even used a few curse words. And of course they then went to my immediate supervisor and filed a complaint. That is how I ended up being sent to see the boss and being forced to come here.

SF Coach: I can see that this is clearly not an easy situation for you and yet clearly you want to keep your job.[14]

Cassandra: I don't just want to – I need to. I don't have anyone else to support me and I have to put in at least two more years before I will qualify for enough benefits to retire.

SF Coach: Obviously keeping this job is important to you. (Client nods). Going back to that scale, let's suppose that you suddenly find yourself at that 7 or 8 and you are now no longer getting deficiency notices. It sounds like these young employees are clearly not likely to change anytime soon, so what will need to happen in order for them to no longer be able to file complaints?

Cassandra: That's a hard question. They are really the ones who should change. They should start planning ahead better about the way they are managing their projects. But they are clearly not likely to change.

SF Coach: Probably not. Given that reality, what does the 7 or 8 look like[15] in terms of how you respond to them? **(SF Scaling Question).**

Cassandra: At a 7 or 8 I wouldn't be getting in to trouble or getting deficiency notices. That would mean that my supervisor would be satisfied that I was behaving correctly. The main thing is that I need to satisfy my supervisor and my boss.

SF Coach: What do you think your supervisor would say you needed to be doing that would indicate to her that you are responding to those young employees in a way that she finds acceptable?

---

[13]When clients express that someone else needs to change in order for things to get better, SF coaches typically express understanding and then ask about the likelihood of the other person being willing to change.

[14]Notice how the SF coach expresses empathy, e.g. *This is clearly not an easy situation* without losing track of the goal.

[15]Asking what a higher position on the scale would *look like* serves to elicit a behavioral description from the client. This is useful because behaviors often prove easier than emotions for clients to consciously replicate.

Cassandra: It's not really fair. They should be the ones who should have to change, not me.

SF Coach: I see what you mean. But as you said, unfortunately that is probably very unlikely to happen anytime soon, and you definitely want to keep your job. Given the realities of this situation, what do you think would need to be different – from your supervisor's perspective – in order for you to be at a 7 or 8 and not have anymore worries about potentially losing your job?

Cassandra: I wouldn't lose my temper. I would just listen to what they needed. I would keep my cool and get it done as soon as I could.

SF Coach: What does it look like when you keep your cool in difficult situations like that? **(SF Detail Question).**

Cassandra: Years ago, I was required to take an anger management course. I learned to silently take several deep breaths and mentally count to 10 before responding to someone who was being obnoxious. People in the class paired up and we practiced staying calm while the other person took turns being obnoxious.

SF Coach: How did that work out for you?

Cassandra: I could definitely do it. But it's harder in real-life situations. And it's harder at this age because sometimes I am really tired. And I get stressed because I want to do a good job.

SF Coach: Understandably.

Cassandra: I wish my old boss was still there.

SF Coach: Of course ... (Client nods). I notice that we are getting pretty close to the end of our time today. Before we end, is there anything else that I should ask or that you think would be important to tell me? **(SF Safety Net Question).**

Cassandra: No, I don't think so.

SF Coach: In that case, I just want to say that the many important technological work skills you obviously have and also your long tenure in your current position all speak volumes about your abilities and your positive attributes as an employee. (Client nods). And I really appreciate your patience in answering my many questions especially since coming here was not your choice. **(SF Direct Compliment).**

Cassandra: Actually is wasn't as bad as I thought it was going to be even though I definitely don't want to be here. I'm just trying to keep my job.

SF Coach: Your boss pre-arranged for you to return for an additional session. Assuming that you decide[16] to do that, I want to offer you a couple of small ideas. Is that okay with you?

---

[16]Like SFT, SFC is characterised by an eminently respectful stance toward the client. Notice how the SF coach is careful to respect that client's position of being the best expert on what she is likely to do, e.g. *assuming that you decide.* And the coach is careful to ask the client's permission before proceeding further, by asking *Is that okay with you?*

Cassandra: Alright.

SF Coach: Between now and next time we meet, I would like to invite you to simply pay attention to anytime when you notice yourself somehow – regardless of what they might be doing – finding creative ways to respond to people in a way that would be consistent with your 7 or 8 position on the scale.

Cassandra: Ok.

Session Ends.

Session 2

The SF coach begins by greeting Cassandra and welcoming her into the office. Once they have taken their chairs, the following conversation takes place:

SF Coach: What's better since last time we met? (SF What's Better Question).

Cassandra: That's a weird way to begin a conversation. I guess one thing that I can honestly say is better is that after this I am only required to come here one more time.

SF Coach: What else is better? (SF What's Better Question).

Cassandra: I didn't get any deficiency notices from my supervisor over the past two weeks.

SF Coach: How do you explain that?

Cassandra: I kept thinking about needing to be at a 7 or 8 on the scale and realised that in order to do that I was going to have to keep my mouth shut and just take down the information when people come into my office and seem to expect me to somehow wave a magic wand to get things done that they should have put in a request for weeks ago.

SF Coach: I can imagine that must be really difficult when that happens. But how exactly did the scale come into it in terms of not getting a deficiency notice?[17]

Cassandra: Like I said. I just kept thinking about needing to be at a 7 or an 8 and that made me remember not to react to people when they were being obnoxious.

SF Coach: That does not sound easy given what you've described. How did you do it – I mean what did you do instead of reacting? (SF Instead Question).

Cassandra: I just listened to them, took their forms, said I would do the best I could, walked right back to my desk, and went back to working on whatever I

---

[17]Notice how the SF coach expresses empathy, i.e. *That must be difficult,* while still remaining focused on the important SF Exception of the client not receiving further deficiency notices.

was already doing. There is a little counter at the front of my office area where they come and leave their filled-out request forms. Usually they spend some time standing there explaining to me why they were so late in dropping it off and why it is so important that it gets done immediately and all that time I have to stand there wasting my time. Usually I try to educate them about why they need to plan better, but this week I quit bothering to do that. It saves me time that way.

SF Coach: How did they seem to respond to this?

Cassandra: At first they would just stand there at the counter waiting. I think they expected me to say something further about their lack of planning, that sort of thing. But as soon as I went back to my desk, they just left. I think that some of them were surprised. One person even thanked me for being 'understanding.'

SF Coach: No deficiency notices over the past two weeks and one person actually thanked you for being so understanding ... Where does that put you on your Confidence scale?

Cassandra: I would say that at the moment I am at a 5 or a 6. It has not been easy. Some of those new employees would drive anyone crazy.

SF Coach: And yet you are somehow managing to be at a 5 or a 6 despite the fact that you describe some of the new employees as people who could drive anyone crazy. How are you managing to cope to the degree that you are now at a 5 or 6? **(SF Coping Question)**.

Cassandra: I didn't say that they weren't driving me crazy. Nothing has really changed regarding that and I don't expect that it will anytime soon, if ever. But I am keeping my eye on the goal post.

SF Coach: The goal post?

Cassandra: You know, how in sports the players have to keep their minds on the goal.

SF Coach: And you are finding it helpful to keep your mind on the goal? (Client nods). How did you figure out that this was something you needed to do? **(SF Indirect Compliment)**.

Cassandra: I assessed the situation I am in, thought about it for a while, and realised that the bottom line was I needed to find a way to survive in this job for the next two years and three days.

SF Coach: You calculated it down to the exact number of years and days? (This is conveyed in a positive, appreciative tone.) **(SF Direct Compliment)**.

Cassandra: I did. And then I checked with the EAP people just to make sure that I was correct in my calculations regarding the exact day I would be eligible for my pension. And I had gotten it precisely right.

SF Coach: Wow, you must be very good at math. **(SF Direct Compliment)**.

Cassandra: I am.

SF Coach: I can clearly see that. **(SF Direct Compliment)**. Is there anything else that has contributed to your now being at a 5 or a 6 in terms of being confident that you will be able to keep your job? **(SF Scaling Question)**.

Cassandra: There is a little personal notepad on my desk with the day's date on it. Once I figured out exactly how many days of work I have left before I can stop working and start collecting my pension, I started writing the remaining number of days on the corner of that day's page of my notepad every morning. No one but me is likely to see it. But even if someone did notice it they probably wouldn't know what the daily number meant. I write out the number of days left each day in really really small letters, so most people who come into my office and stand at the counter waiting to drop-off work would probably never be able to read them anyway.

SF Coach: Writing down that number and seeing it on your little private notepad is clearly part of the 5 or 6. Is there anything else that helps? **(SF What Else Question).**

Cassandra: I am determined to not do anything that would give my supervisor or my boss a reason to fire me. And having some time pass is going to make it easier too, I think.

SF Coach: Your reaching a point at which you feel resolved about this sounds like it has made an important difference.

Cassandra: It has. And writing out the number of days left before I retire on my notepad every day helps too because I can see that I am gradually making progress toward my goal of not needing to be there anymore ...

SF Coach: You also mentioned that having some time pass will be helpful. How will that be helpful?

Cassandra: The more time that passes, the closer I am going to be to getting my pension.

SF Coach: You have clearly given this a lot of thought, and you seem to have become increasingly forward thinking about finding ways to make the situation at work more survivable.

Cassandra: Yes, that is what I have done. I still don't like a lot of what is going on there in terms of office politics and things like that and the way some of the new employees are treating the older, more senior employees, but I am feeling more confident that I can ultimately make it work for the remaining time.

SF Coach: Today, just before you came in, I was looking at my notes from our previous session. Last time you said that a 7 or an 8 would be a good enough number on your Confidence Scale. Does that number still fit for you in terms of how confidence you need to be about ultimately being able to keep your job? **(SF Scaling Question).**

Cassandra: Yes, I would say that is still an accurate number.

SF Coach: I want to make sure that I have correctly understood. You are now at a 5 or a 6 which is a big jump ahead from last time, and your goal is to get to a 7 or an 8 in order to feel sufficiently confident about staying in your current job position for the next two years?

Cassandra: Correct, except it is technically two years and three days.

SF Coach: Let's suppose that one day you find yourself at a 7 or an 8. First of all, what will tell you that you are now at an 8 and how will it have most likely happened? **(SF Scaling Question)**.

Cassandra: That's a hard question ... . (She pauses). First of all, many months will have passed without getting any more deficiency notices or my yelling at the employees for being so disorganised in turning in their requests.

SF Coach: Time will have passed. What else would you notice that will tell you that you are at a 7 or an 8? **(SF Scaling Question)**.

Cassandra: At a 7 or 8 I will start the workday in a better frame of mind. I don't say that I will be in a great mood, but I will be in a reasonably positive kind of mood. For one thing, I won't be making it a point to show up at the office an hour early in order to avoid seeing any other employees or my supervisor or boss.

SF Coach: What will you be doing instead? **(SF Instead Question)**.

Cassandra: I will show up at a normal time, the way I used to when my old boss was there and before there were all these completely disorganised new young employees.

SF Coach: You will show up at a normal time. Let's suppose you are now at a 7 or an 8 and you actually find yourself doing this. How do you suppose people will react? **(SF Scaling Question)**.

Cassandra: They would either not even notice or some of them might say good morning to me.

SF Coach: Let's suppose they say good morning, how will you react at this 7 or 8 position? **(SF Scaling Question)**.

Cassandra: I would just go back to my office. But I might go into the staff lounge first and pour myself a cup of coffee. Usually I miss out on the coffee because I am trying to avoid people.

SF Coach: You would pour yourself a cup of coffee. Would you take it back to your office or drink it in the staff lounge with the others? **(SF Detail Question)**.

Cassandra: It would depend on who was there. And perhaps also whether there were any donuts. Sometimes people bring donuts.

SF Coach: Are donuts part of the 7 or 8? **(SF Detail Question)**.

Cassandra: This probably sounds weird, but actually I think that donuts ARE part of the 7 or 8.

SF Coach: Makes sense to me. So, before we end today, is there anything else that I should ask or that would be important for us to talk about?

Cassandra: I don't think so.

SF Coach: In that case, I just want to tell you how impressed I am with how clear you are about what you need to do and the fact that you went up several points on your scale in the past two weeks. And I have one small idea I can offer if you are interested.

Cassandra: Okay.

SF Coach: My idea is for you to simply pay attention to anything that you do that is either part of the 7 or 8, that helps you move in the direction of the 7 or 8 or even higher, and of course anything you do that you find helpful in preventing your number from getting lower. Does that make sense?

Cassandra: It does. My boss said I do not need to come back again after this session unless you think that I need to. Do I need to?

SF Coach: I am of course always happy to meet with you in the future if you think it would be helpful, but the decision would be completely up to you. It has been a pleasure to work with you.

Cassandra: I can't say that it has been a pleasure for me to come here, but it has not been at all as bad as I expected it to be.

SF Coach: I am very glad to hear that. Is there anything I could have done that would have made it a better experience for you or is there anything else that would be important for me to ask before we finish today? **(SF Safety Net Question).**

Cassandra: Not really. It was as good as it could be under the circumstances.

SF Coach: Glad to hear that also. And please do not hesitate to call for an appointment if at some point you think it might be helpful.

Cassandra: Thanks.

SESSION ENDS.

Session Follow-Up

About six weeks after the previous session, the SF coach received the following phone message from Cassandra's boss:

I know you can't tell me what went on in those sessions with Cassandra, but I really wish you could. After seeing you she immediately started getting along better with her co-workers. And yesterday her supervisor told me that Cassandra brought a big box of donuts to the staff lounge. People were stunned. We didn't know what to think, but things are differently better; she has not received any further deficiency notices.

Two years later the SF coach, now serving as a part-time staff consultant for the company's employees, received the following email from one of the secretaries at Cassandra's company:

The company is throwing a farewell party for Cassandra and she specifically requested that you receive an invitation.

Although the SF Coach was very busy that week, she promised to drop in for at least a few minutes. While there, she witnessed the following exchange between Cassandra and one of the younger employees.

Young Employee: We are going to miss you, Cassandra! It won't be the same here without you coming in first thing in the morning and starting the coffee.
Cassandra: I wish I could say I was going to miss coming in to work, but I can't say I will. I'm going to be home enjoying not having to get up early in the morning. But I do appreciate you telling me this.

DISCUSSION

As is likely evident, the SFC sessions did not change Cassandra's somewhat gruff, abrupt communication style. But they helped her to develop the kind of solution necessary to retain her job. While the SF coach deliberately refrains from interpreting the "meaning" behind a client's behavior or offering proscriptive directions, SFC clients typically start showing significant behavioral changes on their own as evidenced by Cassandra. Perhaps this is linked to the fact that people are oftentimes more readily willing to embrace new behaviors that they identify themselves rather than those recommended by so-called professional "experts."

Here is a general overview of how the SF approach was employed in Cassandra's two coaching sessions: After it became clear that Cassandra did not want to participate in coaching sessions and had no desire to return for further sessions, the SF Coach respectfully communicated empathy by responding that Cassandra was in a *difficult position*. The coach further demonstrated positive intent by asking Cassandra what the session needed to focus on in order to possibly prove useful rather than a waste of time. Over the course of the two sessions, the SF coach repeatedly incorporated Cassandra's exact words into various responses. This served to communicate respect and convey accurate understanding.

While SF coaches do not hesitate to express empathy, they generally develop rapport by focusing on the client's strengths. This was exemplified by the SF coach's detailed questions about what Cassandra did well in her job. While it is typical for SF coaches to ask questions designed to generate descriptions of previous experiences evidencing their clients' strengths and resources, this was especially essential for establishing a working relationship with a person like Cassandra; she was essentially an involuntary client in that she was coming to the coaching sessions solely because her boss required her to do so. And while asking what Cassandra was good at in her job contributed to developing rapport, it also served an important additional purpose: Resources and strengths uncovered in response to this question are essential to the solution-development process.

SF coaches oftentimes explain the purpose for asking SF questions before introducing them. This can be especially important when utilising the SFC approach with clients like Cassandra who might otherwise worry about the motive behind a question, or that their response might later be used as rationale for demoting or firing them. The first SF Scaling Question that the SF coach asks Cassandra is therefore carefully prefaced with, *Is it okay if I ask you a question in order to better understand?* This communicates that the question is unlikely to be adversarial and that the coach's intent is positive.

There is an interesting interaction between the SF coach and Cassandra during the process of answering the SF Scaling Question that clearly illustrates one of the hallmarks of the SF approach and clearly differentiates it from problem-focused approaches. Describing what contributed to rating herself at 2 ½ on the scale, Cassandra discloses that she has recently received some deficiency notices. At this juncture a coach working from a problem-focused model would have likely begun exploring the details of the problem indicated by the deficiency notices. But the SF coach stays focused on the solution-development process by responding, *Let's suppose you were no longer receiving deficiency letters. What number would that put you on the scale?*

Despite the fact that Cassandra is initially reluctant to engage in the coaching, the SF coach does not hesitate to offer SF Direct and Indirect Compliments related to Cassandra's accomplishments as they gradually become evident. By the conclusion of the second session, Cassandra has clearly made significant strides in the direction of keeping her job, and the SF coach simply encourages her to continue this process on her own by P*aying attention to anything that is either part of the 7 or 8, helps you move in the direction of the 7 or 8 or even higher, and/or anything you do that you find helpful in preventing your number from getting lower.*

CHAPTER SUMMARY

The SFC process is indistinguishable from the SFT process except for the fact that SFC is limited to contexts related to clients' professional aspirations. The SFC approach is demonstrated with transcripts which illustrate what the approach looks like with two different clients: A recently terminated executive trying to regain his confidence in order to seek new employment and a disgruntled employee seeking to avoid getting fired.

EXPERIENTIAL SF EXERCISE: PROFESSIONAL ASPIRATIONS

Take a few moments to think about your ideal work situation.
What sort of work does this involve?
What is your ideal work setting?
Would you ideally work alone or with co-workers?
What constitutes your ideal working relationship (if applicable)?
Let's suppose you had a job that ideally reflected all of the previous items. What would that look like?

Imagine a 0–10 scale in which 10 represents your ideal job and 0 represents the Opposite. Where would you currently rate yourself of this scale? What contributes to this number not being lower? Let's suppose you found that you have gone up a point on your Scale. What would that look like? In the next few days, pay attention to anything that you do (or someone else does) that contributes to you moving (even in a small way) in the direction of the ideal 10.

REFERENCES

Grant, A. M. (2012). Making positive change: A randomized study comparing solution-focused vs. problem-focused coaching questions. *Journal of Systemic Therapies, 31*(2), 21–35.

Grant, A. M., & Gerrard, B. (2020). Comparing problem-focused, solution-focused and combined problem-focused/solution-focused coaching approach: Solution-focused coaching questions mitigate the negative impact of dysfunctional attitudes. *Coaching: An International Journal of Theory, Research and Practice, 13*(1), 61–77.

Hogan, D. (2017). Work Smarter, Not Harder. In D. Hogan, D. Hogan, J. Tuomola, & Alan Yeo, (Eds.), *Solution-focused practice in Asia.* New York: Routledge, pp. 247–255.

Iveson, C., George, E., & Rather, H. (2012). *Brief coaching: A Solution-focused approach.* New York: Routledge.

Rather, H., George, E., & Iveson, C. (2012). *Solution-focused brief therapy: 100 key points and techniques.* New York: Routledge.

Szabo, P., & Meier, D. (2009). *Coaching plain & simple: Solution-focused brief coaching essentials.* New York, NY: W W Norton & Co.

Theeboom, T., Beersma, B., & Van Vianen, A. E. M. (2016). The differential effects of solution-focused and problem-focused coaching questions on the affect, attentional control and cognitive flexibility of undergraduate students experiencing study-related stress. *The Journal of Positive Psychology*, *11*(5), 460–469.

SOLUTION-FOCUSED THERAPY APPLIED TO SELF-HELP

Numerous books have been written about applying the SFT approach to self-help for a variety of purposes. These include enhancing quality of life (Dolan, 2000; Duncan, 2005; Gibson, 2020; Ghul, 2015; Hudson, 1996; Metcalf, 2004; O'Hanlon, 2004; Weiner-Davis, 1996), thriving after trauma (Dolan, 2000; Henden 2011; 2017; Scott et al., 2021), overcoming substance use disorder (Berg & Miller, 1997), weight loss (Dolan, 1997), and improving couple relationships (Connie, 2013; Weiner-Davis, 1992).

SF self-help techniques typically have a calming, soothing effect. They foster positive emotions which naturally interrupt upsetting thought patterns (von Cziffra-Bergs, 2018, p. 57), provide a context of hope (Dolan, 1991, p. 40), and function as a natural counterbalance or "antidote" to painful or disturbing feelings (Bannick, 2014, p. 7).

Of the various SF techniques, the SF Miracle or Best Hope Question, Coping Questions, and SF Scaling and SF Exception Questions are the most readily adaptable to self-help. This chapter provides detailed examples of how these popular techniques can be employed to enhance one's quality of life and cope with challenging circumstances, and it also describes how one can live a solution-focused lifestyle. An experiential SF self-help exercise is included at the end of the chapter.

JESSICA: ENHANCING EVERYDAY QUALITY OF LIFE

While growing up in a series of temporary foster homes, Jessica repeatedly vowed to create a better, happier life when she grew up. Immediately following high school graduation, she enlisted in the

DOI: 10.4324/9781003401230-7

military. After completing military service, she immediately enrolled in a local university where she earned a business accounting degree that had led to her current job at a large corporation.

Hard working and determined to succeed, Jessica received a promotion at the end of her first year on the job. A naturally frugal person, after two years she had managed to save enough money to purchase a small house. In purchasing her new home, Jessica had completed all of the personal and professional goals that had guided her life since adolescence, e.g. find a way to fund college, earn a college degree, get a job, and buy a home. Having succeeded with everything she had set out to do, Jessica wondered why was she did not feel happier. Although reasonably content with her everyday life, she rarely experienced joy or even a sense of deep satisfaction.

Although she wanted to feel happier in her everyday life, Jessica felt reluctant to set up an appointment with a counselor having already attended numerous appointments with social workers, school guidance counselors, and psychotherapists during a childhood and adolescence spent in a series of foster care homes. Deciding to pursue self-help options, she picked up a self-help book written by an SF practitioner. The following weekend, Jessica begin flipping through the pages of the book while she sipped her morning coffee.

Pragmatic by nature, Jessica was immediately drawn to an SF Self-Scaling technique utilising a 0–10 scale in which 10 represented one's Best Hope and 0 represented the Opposite. But then she realised that she was not sure what her best hope was other than wanting to experience more joy in her everyday life.

How do you help yourself if you are not sure of any of the specifics of your goal or even your best hope? she wondered. Having grown up in a series of chaotic foster living situations, she knew exactly what she *didn't* want: Uncertainty, disorganisation, over-crowded living conditions, chaos, a pervasive feeling of loneliness. But what *did* she want? Although Jessica did not feel like she should be constantly happy, she did want to feel more joyous and satisfied in her everyday life. But what did that really mean?

Quickly scanning the book, Jessica read about the SF Miracle Question and discovered that it been originally designed for situations in which some or all of the details of a hope or goal might initially be unclear or perhaps even seemingly impossible:

> *Let's suppose that tonight you go to sleep and sometime while you are sleeping a Miracle happens. It is a very particular kind of 'Miracle' in which your best hope has suddenly been fulfilled in the best possible way. But since you were asleep when it happened, you do not realize that the Miracle has happened until you after you wake up and begin going about your day.*
>
> *What would be the first things that would be different on the day after the Miracle that you or other people might notice that would tell you that something had changed? This question requires some imagination and quite a bit of concentration, so make sure to give yourself as much time as necessary to answer.* **(SF Miracle Question).**

Finding a pencil and notepad, Jessica made a commitment not to censor or criticise herself but to just write whatever came to mind. Here is what came out:

> *On the first morning after the Miracle: I wake up with a plan for the day that involves seeing other people. It also involves leaving the house and spending sometimes outdoors. I get out of bed and I walk to the refrigerator where I find some fresh fruit, I make a good cup of coffee and eat a nice breakfast And I feel happy about how I plan to spend the day.*
>
> *Walking to my garage, I see a border of pink flowers that look like the ones I remember seeing at my best friends' house when I was in Middle School. There are not any weeds next to my sidewalk, just flowers.*
>
> *I get into my car and notice that it has been freshly washed inside and outside. I plug in my phone and listen to a favorite piece of music that I stored on it. Then I leave for work. But I am taking a different route than usual because I have left the house early enough to drive by the park and spend a little bit of time watching the ducks in the pond. I have brought some leftover bread pieces which I watch them eat. I am wearing a blue dress in my absolute favorite color. There are a few joggers at the park but I do not pay any attention to the joggers. I am just concentrating on spending time watching the ducks and the little ducklings moving around the pond. I just relax and watch them for a while. I toss them a few little pieces of bread, get back into my car and leave for work. My car is nice and clean and it smells good. I am wearing a dress in my favorite color of blue and I have packed a nice lunch to eat at my desk later.*
>
> *When I arrive at work, my co-workers probably notice that I have a smile on my face although they do not say anything directly to me. In my office, I get right to work but in the back of my mind I am thinking about my new friend and (I think I may have met a potential partner!) and what we are planning to do this weekend.*
>
> *After work, I don't go home right away. I do something fun like meeting someone for coffee or attending one of the after-work concerts in the park.*

When I get home, I fix a fresh healthy dinner composed of things that I like (probably a really nice salad) because I have managed to lose the extra weight I had been carrying and I don't want to gain it back. All my clothing is feeling loose and comfortable and that makes me very happy. I take my dinner outside and sit at a little table that is placed right next to the pink flowers. There are butterflies and birdsongs and they make me smile.

The neighbor's cat comes over and lets me pet her. This really would be a miracle because she is normally aloof! She rubs against my legs making a rumbly purring sound that I really enjoy. That night I have a nice telephone conversation before I go to bed. (Since it's a Miracle, I now have someone special that I talk to on the phone, someone who is potentially interested in a long-term relationship, and I feel hopeful about the possibilities)

My sheets and bedding are fresh and clean and my room smells like lavender because I have placed a bowl of dried lavender sitting on the night table like I have sometimes seen in magazines. I have furnished and decorated my house in a way that reflects the person I want to be — the person I am deep inside, and that makes me happy.

I listen to the sound of ocean waves before I go to sleep (Even though I live far from the ocean, this is a Miracle (!) So I can hear the waves. I feel good in my body and I drift off to sleep knowing that I am safe and warm and truly happy in a more joyous sense.

The instructions in the self-help book suggest that:

Once the description of the day after the Miracle has been completed, draw a 0–10 scale in which 10 represents how things are after miracle has happened and 0 represents the complete opposite.

So now Jessica draws the scale and takes a moment to think. The author of the self-help book has written that:

Some aspects of the Miracle are likely already present in your life to some degree, or have perhaps been previously present in your life to some extent. These are called Exceptions. Think of those exceptions and decide where you are currently on your Miracle Scale.

Jessica looks at the 0–10 scale that she has drawn and makes a mark over a space approximately 2 points to the right of the zero. *It is a 2,* she decides. The 2 reflects the fact that she does have a job and a car and that she owns some nice sheets and bedding even if they have not been recently washed. And although she has not had a romantic partner of any kind for over a year now, she does have a friend that she could telephone. But there are no flowers in her yard, the neighbors cat typically ignores her and the only food in her refrigerator is stale leftovers from fast-food places. And there is no potential partner calling or texting her. Sighing, Jessica returns to reading the instructions in the SF self-help book.

> *Think of at least one small thing that you could reasonably do in the next 24 hours to raise your current number on your Miracle Scale.*

Jessica sighs. She is not sure that this is going to work. But after a few moments, she rises slowly from her chair, walks into the bedroom, strips the sheets and pillow cases off her bed, places them into the washing machine, adds soap, and starts the wash cycle. Then she goes back to the table, refills her coffee cup, opens her computer, and goes to an online site where she orders a package of dried lavender. It is a Saturday morning, so she decides to visit a local secondhand shop to look for a pretty bowl for the lavender. She finds nothing. But then she decides to visit a local garden store where she purchases several containers of pink geraniums and a big bag of garden soil.

Following that, Jessica stops at the local supermarket and purchases some fresh fruit and vegetables. She returns home, leaves the pink geraniums on the front porch, and carries the bag of groceries into the house. Opening the refrigerator, her nose is assailed by the disgusting smell of stale food. She collects all the fast-food containers, throws them into a garbage, and carries it to the outside trashcan.

While outside, she sees the neighbors' beautiful cat and calls out to him. But the cat simply ignores her as usual. Back inside the house, Jessica wipes down the refrigerator shelves with hot soapy water and switches on some music. When the refrigerator looks and smells pleasingly clean, Jessica wipes all the surfaces one more time, places the fresh fruit inside, and puts away the remaining groceries.

Then she removes a ripe mango from the refrigerator. She peels and eats it at the kitchen table. Noticing that the scale she drew two hours ago is still there, Jessica crosses out the 2, and makes a mark at the 2 ½ position. Although not exactly feeling joyous, she notices herself feeling a little bit lighter, a little bit more like smiling. *Is this a mental or a physical or mental phenomenon,* she wonders. Jessica doesn't know and she doesn't care.

Then she picks up her cell phone and calls her friend to whom she has not spoken in several days. They have a nice conversation. Afterwards, she goes outside, knocks on the neighbor's door and asks to borrow a shovel. Back in her yard a few minutes later, she proceeds to plant the flowers and pours water over them. Then she starts pulling up the masses of weeds that have inserted themselves along her sidewalk.

Jessica is surprised by how much time has passed by the time she finishes the weeding. Remembering the sheets still in the washing machine, she places them in the dryer, showers while they are drying, and then changes the bedding. She and her bed are now both completely clean and her refrigerator is filled with healthy food. She resists the temptation to go to the local fast-food place and prepares a salad instead. That night she sleeps slightly better. When she wakes up, she notices that she is still not joyous. But she is definitely feeling at least a tiny bit better than she did two days ago, so she resolves to keep using the Miracle scale.

On Monday morning, Jessica gets up a little bit earlier than usual and finds that she has a little bit of extra time because she packed today's lunch last night. Feeling less rushed and pressured than useful, she brews a cup of coffee and settles down to a pleasant breakfast of toast and fresh fruit. Noticing several pink geraniums blooming outside her window, Jessica stops to water them before leaving for work and enjoys their subtle scent.

In the car, she plugs in her cell phone and finds a selection of favorite music which she listens to while driving to the park. Although she does not have much extra time, Jessica manages to feed the ducks some bread crumbs. Pulling out of the parking space a few minutes later, Jessica finds herself smiling and decides that she is now at a 4 on her scale.

She wonders what makes it a 4? Is it the sunshine, the ducks, the pink flowers, the fruit, the fact that she packed a nice lunch? She isn't sure; perhaps it is all of these things together, or maybe it is simply the effect of using the SF scale to monitor her self-care and follow her intention to become more joyous.

As Jessica walks through the office reception area, her friend, Grace, gives her a speculative look. "*Who is he,*" she asks humorously, "*I mean the person who put that smile on your face?*" "*You clearly have a very active imagination,*" replies Jessica as she breezes past Grace's desk. But Jessica knows that somehow her mood is a little bit lighter than usual. During her lunch break, Jessica tries to think of what might raise her number a little further on her Miracle; she remembers the description she wrote of the Miracle Day.

She thinks of the blue dress that she imagined in response to the Miracle question, but she remembers that she is on a budget. A few days earlier, Jessica had purchased an inexpensive "sleep machine" that plays recorded sounds of waves lapping against the shore. She thinks it might be improving the quality of her sleep. Although she sometimes envies friends who share living expenses with a partner or roommate, Jessica currently appreciates the quiet and privacy of living alone.

The SF Letter from the Future

That night Jessica starts reading the SF self-help book again and finds an exercise called the SF Miracle Letter from the Future (Dolan, 2000).

> *Imagine that some time has passed (whatever number of days, months, or years you choose) and you are now living exactly as you envisioned when you answered the Miracle question based on your best hopes. Think of a person in your life who would be happy to hear that things are going well for you. Write a future dated letter to them describing in detail what you have been doing, how you have been spending your time and describing any positive changes that have occurred since last time you communicated. (This letter is not intended to be sent; it's purpose is to provide further clarity and realism to your Miracle description. If you can envision it, doing it becomes more accessible).*

Jessica tries to think of someone who would be happy to hear that things were going well for her. This proves to be difficult at first; Jessica tends to keep most of the people in her everyday life at a distance. But then she thinks of Mrs. Armstrong, her former high school guidance counselor; Jessica has never forgotten Mrs. Armstrongs's words.

> *You are way too hard on yourself, Jess. You have every right to be proud of how well you are doing in your classes. You are a very nice person with a good heart and you are also very determined and hardworking. Some day your ship is going to come in and when it does, remember that I told you this.*

Mrs. Armstrong would be pleased to hear her prediction had proven true. Jessica finds a pen and leafs through an old notebook until she finds an empty page. On the top right hand corner, she writes a future date exactly three years from now. After several stops and starts, she writes the following:

> *Dear Mrs. Armstrong,*
> *I hope you are well. You were the best school counselor I ever knew.*

I thought you would like to know that my ship has finally come in. I got my university degree, found a decent job that I like well enough, and I now have my own little house where I live with my cat and my partner.

My partner is really nice. We met at a book signing for one of my favorite authors, a wild life researcher who writes about the hidden lives of the animals who populate National Parks.

Given how much I liked high school science classes, you will probably not be surprised to hear that I gradually began spending more and more time visiting beautiful outdoor places around the country and have spent my summer vacations volunteering at the local National Park. You would be surprised by how physically fit I have become!

I have spent part of the past three summers living in a tent while volunteering at a wild-life refuge. (Our neighbor takes care of my cat whenever I am away and I return the favor by caring for hers whenever she leaves town). I have installed a self-watering drip system in my garden to keep things blooming during the weeks when I am away. I love my garden! And I did it myself so it didn't cost much!

I am thinking that I would like to become a parent someday, and that I would like to adopt a child who might otherwise end up in a series of foster homes like I did.

I think you once told me that you had adopted both your children. I am trying to become the kind of person that an adoption agency would consider to be a good parent, eg. living a healthy life style, making enough money to support a child, and behaving like a person who is reasonably sane (whatever that means)! I have already saved quite a bit of money toward the costs involved in adopting a child, I feel hopeful about the future and even sometimes very joyous about my everyday life, especially when spending time outside.

Thank you from the bottom of my heart for all the help and support you gave me in High School. I truly don't know what I would have done without you. Jessica.

Jessica tears the page out of the notebook and rereads what she has written. Folding the paper into thirds, she places it in an envelope and carefully tucks it at the bottom of a drawer underneath her socks.

Feeling somewhat surprised by what she has written, she finds herself wondering:

*Was **this** the Miracle that she wanted?*

Deciding that she is still at a 4 on the Miracle scale Jessica wonders what else she might do to raise her number.

A couple of weeks later, she sees her neighbor in the backyard. The neighbor mentions that she is going to be out of town for a few days and wonders if Jessica would be willing to feed her cat while she is away. Jessica surprises herself by immediately offering to do this. During the neighbor's absence, the cat becomes slightly more friendly and Jessica realises that she will miss having daily contact with the animal.

A month later, Jessica finds herself driving to the local animal shelter to adopt a cat of her own. Now at a 5 on her scale, she notices that her clothes have become comfortably loose. Perhaps this is due to increasingly eating the fresh, healthy foods that she imagined while writing about her imaginary Miracle, or maybe it is from the physical exercise she has been getting while working in her little garden.

It takes several days for Jessica's newly adopted cat to adjust to living in the house. Although Jessica has decided to keep the cat indoors for safety, she is saddened to see it constantly looking longingly out the window. This leads to a decision to attach a safely screened and enclosed outdoor "cat space" so her pet can safely venture outside.

Despite hiring a professional carpenter, it takes several weeks to complete this project. But on the day that her cat ventures into the new safely enclosed outdoor "cat run" for the first time, Jessica watches it roll around on the grass. decides it is likely feeling joyful, a feeling she now recognises in herself. That weekend, Jessica invited a few friends from work to come over on Saturday night to meet her cat and share a potluck meal. Her neighbor comes, too.

That night Jessica wears a new blue dress in the same color that she envisioned in response to the Miracle Question. As she is preparing for bed at the end of the evening, Jessica realises that she is now at a 7 ½ on her scale. Drifting off to sleep a few moment later, she wonders what she will need to do to maintain that number, and is surprised by the gentle, dream-like images that spontaneously come to mind.

Sitting outside sipping her morning coffee the following day watching the cat enjoy its new outdoor abode, Jessica wonders if maintaining the 7 ½ may ultimately prove easier than she might have expected. She is surprised by the realisation that many of the things that contribute to the 7 ½ have proven to be relatively simple. Spending time outside, enjoying the company of her cat, eating well, and reaching out to friends are things that contribute significantly to her quality of life. Further, even just contemplating these simple activities has sometimes led to a sense of joyous anticipation and appreciation. Jessica wonders if some of these moments of joy have occurred in the past but somehow went unnoticed. Perhaps self-scaling has made her more attentive to them?

Later in the week during a break in her workday, Jessica asks herself *what would it take to get to an 8?* That night she opens her computer and begins exploring weekend volunteer possibilities on the internet. She finds several requests for weekend volunteers at the local parks and recreation department that interest her. She chooses one and sends in her application.

A year later, Jessica has been volunteering at the children's playground at the local park two weekends a month for a year when she begins to think of the possibility of becoming a single parent. Although she has been hoping to meet someone special for a long time, and to have a family of her own, Jessica feels 0% attraction to any of the men she currently knows and does not want to pursue online dating sites.

Exactly two years later, Jessica fills out an adoption application. At this point she has attended a series of parenting classes, spent a lot of time thinking about whether she was ready to take on the responsibility of parenthood, and saved up the necessary money.

By now, Jessica has been volunteering at the local park playground and a wildlife center on a regular basis. She has found many kindred spirits among the other volunteers, all of whom attend the baby shower organised by Jessica's friends and co-workers.

After signing the final adoption papers, Jessica tenderly cuddles her little boy and decides that at least for today, she is definitely at a 10 on her scale. Although Jessica recognises that there will inevitably be ups and downs in the future, she also knows what joy feels like and feels hopeful about the future.

Five years later, Jessica continues to use SF scaling to maintain and improve the quality of her everyday life (joy enhancement) and generate creative ideas at work. She recently made the following observation:

> My life is not perfect — no one has a perfect life. But my little family (me, my son, Mittens the cat, and a circle of special friends) continues to provide me with a lot of joy. The SF Miracle Question and SF Scaling helped me discover what I wanted and needed in order to have a happier life. I am still open to meeting the right person, but I no longer feel like my life is on hold and that I won't feel joy until it happens.

DISCUSSION

Did the SF Miracle Question and SF Self-Scaling technique change Jessica? Not exactly. Jessica used the Miracle Question and Self-Scaling to empower herself to discover what would help her move toward finding the sense of joy for which she had been longing.

Oftentimes one of the more challenging aspects of using SF to enhance personal quality of life is figuring out what one actually wants and identifying the first of a series of small practical steps that would signify movement in that direction. The SF Miracle or Best Hope Question and the SF Letter from the Future invite people to use their imaginations and think "outside the box" in order to explore what achieving their goals, hopes, and dreams might look like in everyday life. And SF Scaling provides an efficient way to identify the small behavioral steps needed to gradually move in the direction of a more fulfilling and satisfying everyday life. Jessica utilised all of these with patience and tenacity to create a more joyous life for herself.

Celia: *Self-Care during a Highly Stressful Time*

Six months after Celia and her husband celebrated their 30th wedding anniversary, he was diagnosed with Alzheimer's Disease. An illness for which there is currently no known cure, Alzheimer's Disease is characterised by progressive loss of memory, thinking skills, and the ability to carry out activities of everyday living. Strongly committed to personally caring for her husband at home, Celia sought out all available resources to provide him with the best possible care. Although the couple's adult children and extended family immediately rallied around them and Celia took advantage of the many resources offered by the Alzheimer's Association,[1] managing her husband's care became progressively more challenging as time went on and the disease progressed.

Although deeply committed to providing the best possible care for the man she had loved for all of her adult life, Celia struggled to cope with feelings of profound loss when her husband's memory gradually declined to the point that he no longer recognised her. Already well informed about self-care strategies and committed

---

[1] www.alz.org

to maintaining her physical health, the increased demands of caregiving nevertheless made it increasingly difficult to find time to do many of the things that had previously proved helpful: Meditation, physical exercise, healthy eating, reaching out to others, attending support groups. Not surprisingly, as time went on, Celia found herself feeling increasingly overwhelmed and depleted.

Even reaching out to longtime friends became increasingly more difficult as her husband's care began to require nearly all of her time and energy. Despite her best efforts to cope, Celia gradually found herself feeling increasingly isolated and exhausted, struggling to cope with the ever increasing demands of full-time caregiving while grieving the loss of the person she remembered her husband to have been. In desperation, she reached out to the Alzheimer's Association Helpline[2] where the SF practitioner social worker introduced her to an SF Self-Scaling Question geared to self-care:

Imagine a scale between 0–10 in which 10 represents an Ideal Level of Self Care and 0 signifies the Opposite. Where would you rate yourself today?

Rating herself at a 1 on the Self-Care scale led to Celia's realisation that she needed to start taking better care of herself in order to cope with the stress. Using an SF Scale to assess her current level of Self-Care allowed her to develop further clarity about what was and was not realistic for her given situation. While a 10 represented the ideal, a 6 or a 7 would likely be a "good enough" number to sustain her. When the telephone hotline counselor gently asked,

Let's suppose you went up a point on your Self-Care Scale, what would that look like?

Celia responded that

I would make sure to take time to put on clean clothes each day and manage to sit down for at least one actual meal. (I've been living on snack food).

As she reflected on her SF self-care scale, Celia realised that in addition to inadvertently abandoning many of her normal healthy eating habits, she had become increasingly socially isolated during the past year and that this was having a detrimental effect on her mood. When the social worker described local support groups that variously met either online or in person, Celia decided that

---

[2]Alzheimer's Association 24/7 Helpline (800-272-3900)

attending one might prove helpful and would likely raise her number at least 1/2 a point.

After that telephone conversation, Celia begin using her self-care scale first thing in the morning and last thing at night, rating her current position on the scale, thinking about small everyday things that she might possibly do to variously help herself maintain the current number or possibly raise it during the next several hours. This led to Celia initiating more frequent telephone contact with supportive friends and becoming more vigilant about remembering to eat healthy meals and snacks. Establishing more frequent telephone contact with longtime friends and eating more regularly raised Celia's number on her self-care scale two full points. And self-scaling at the beginning and end of each day helped her remember to take better care of herself.

The next time Celia contacted the hotline, she talked to another SF caregiver consultant who asked her about what she had found helpful so far. When Celia described herself as being currently being at a 5 on a 0–10 scale in which 10 represented her ideal level of self-care and 0 represented the opposite, the counselor asked her what a 6 or 7 might look like. Celia responded:

> I would arrange for a respite caregiver to come in once a week so I can go out and do errands or perhaps meet a friend for lunch.

Following this phone call, Celia drew an image of the self-care scale on a piece of paper and posted it in on the refrigerator door to further serve as a reminder to continue to take care of herself while caring for her husband. Thinking about what might raise her number on the scale led her to reach out to members of her extended family to enlist their help. Having family members come over to the house two evenings a week gave Celia new self-care options. She could occasionally meet friends for dinner, attend a yoga class, or shop for necessities in person rather than having them delivered.

Repeatedly asking the daily self-care scaling question gradually led her to re-establish some small everyday rituals that had proved helpful for staying centered and calm earlier in her life: An afternoon cup of herbal tea, arranging for the delivery of small weekly bouquet by a local florist, scenting her pillow with lavender before she went to bed. It seemed to her that the lavender had a calming effect on her husband as well.

After Celia's husband eventually passed away, she volunteered at a caregiver's peer support organisation. She also participated in a local grief support group. Over time, Celia taught many other people in both those organisations how to use a daily SF self-care scale. Years later, Celia reflected that:

> For me, that scale gradually came to function as an ongoing lifeline that helped me figure out how to cope on a day to basis with the highly stressful realities of caring for a loved one suffering from a progressively degenerative brain disease. Self-scaling helped me be a better caregiver.

> What I learned from self-scaling is that no matter how difficult a day a person is having, there is always at least one small thing that you can do to take care of yourself a little bit better; searching for those little things that help even a little bit invites personal creativity and promotes a more positive mindset.

DISCUSSION

Because the demands and complexities of ongoing caregiving and other challenging situations oftentimes change from day to day, coping strategies need to be flexible. Utilising an SF self-care scale is a readily accessible way for people to regularly monitor their own well-being and generate highly personalised healthy coping strategies while dealing with challenging situations.

The Solution-Focused Lifestyle

Over the years, longtime SF Practitioners attending the author's SF training groups have described themselves as living a **Solution-Focused Lifestyle** (Pichot & Dolan, 2003) in which they consciously apply the SF approach to their personal lives. As one person described:

> Asking myself the Miracle Question in reference to my best hopes revealed what I really wanted, but using the Miracle Scale on an ongoing basis has transformed my life. Putting my goals on an SF Scale in which 10 meant that the Miracle had been achieved and 0 meant the opposite helped me to begin taking practical steps in the direction of creating and preserving a way of life that reflects what matters most to me.

> Even if I don't achieve everything in my personal miracle, asking myself that SF scaling question every morning ensures that I am living in a way that reflects my best hopes and heartfelt beliefs. Basically the SF miracle question helps me figure out what I want in my heart, and SF Scaling helps me use my head to get it by forcing me to use my head by thinking in a logical, step-by-step manner. Each day, I get out of bed and ask myself what small thing I can do or continue doing today in order to move, even a little bit, in the direction of my personal miracle.

In addition to using the **Miracle or Best Hope Question** and **Self-Scaling,** people who describe themselves as living an SF Lifestyle oftentimes say that they find it helpful to remind themselves of the SF assumption, *If it's not working, do something different* to generate productive experimentation. This principle can be applicable to a wide variety of endeavors ranging from the creative arts to educational, scientific and technical fields.

Others have variously expressed that reminding themselves that *no problem happens to the same degree all the time, there are always exceptions* has helped them to endure challenging life circumstances (illness, loss, adversity). Even small exceptions can sometimes contribute to making very difficult situations a bit more bearable by shifting the focus away from everything that is wrong to at least one small thing that is somewhat positive or good.

DISCUSSION

Indeed the SF "Lifestyle" holds virtually unlimited possibilities for creative personal applications and will likely continue to evolve as long as the worldwide popularity and utilisation of the SF approach endures. While a wider discussion of the utilisation of SF Self-Help techniques is beyond the scope of this book, there are numerous resources available as evidenced by the various citations and references which appear at the end of this chapter.

CHAPTER SUMMARY

The SFT approach has been successfully applied to a wide variety of self-help topics including thriving after trauma (Dolan, 1998, 2000; Henden, 2011; Henden, 2017; Scott et al., 2021), overcoming substance use disorder (Berg & Miller, 1997), improving couple relationships (O'Hanlon and Hudson, 1995; Connie, 2013; Weiner-Davis, 1992), and others. Popular SF self-help techniques include asking oneself the **SF Miracle Question,** Self-Scaling, and the **SF Miracle Letter from the Future.** People who become familiar with SF self-help techniques sometimes subsequently describe themselves as living a "solution-focused lifestyle" in which they periodically ask themselves the SF Miracle Question or write an SF Miracle Letter from the Future to envision creative solutions. Some people use daily **SF Self-Scaling** to cope with ongoing stress. Others use SF Self-Scaling to formulate practical behavioral steps to move in the direction of their best hopes.

Experiential Exercise

1. **Answer the SF Miracle Question**

   Let's suppose that tonight you go to sleep and sometime during the night a sort of Miracle happens while you are sleeping. It is a very particular kind of "Miracle" in which your best hope has suddenly been fulfilled in the best possible way. But since you were asleep when it happened, you do not realize that the Miracle has happened until you after you wake up and begin your day.

   What would be the first thing(s) that would be different on the day after the Miracle that you or other people might notice that would tell you that something had changed? This question requires some imagination and quite a bit of concentration, so make sure to give yourself as much time as necessary to answer.

2. **Write[3] the SF Miracle Letter from the Future:**

   Imagine that some time has passed (whatever number of days, months, or years you choose) and you are now living exactly as you envisioned when you answered the Miracle question based on your best hopes. Think of a person in your life who would be happy to hear that things are going well for you. Write a future dated letter to them describing in detail what you have been doing, how you have been spending your time, and describing any positive changes that have occurred since the last time you communicated. (This letter is not intended to be sent; its purpose is to provide further clarity and realism to your Miracle description).

3. **Use the SF Miracle Scale:**

   Once you have written the SF Miracle Letter, draw a 0–10 scale in which 10 represents that you are currently living the life described in the SF Miracle Letter and 0 represents the complete opposite. Typically some aspects of the Miracle are already present in your life at least to some degree, or have perhaps been previously present in your life to some degree. These are called Exceptions. Think of those exceptions and decide where you are currently on your Miracle Scale. Then use the scale to identify the next small step needed to move in the direction of your Miracle. You can continue to formulate additional next small steps as often as helpful in order to continue to progress toward your goal.

---

[3]As an alternative to writing the letter, people sometimes create an auditory recording based on how they imagine describing the changes that have occurred in their life to a supportive listener at a time in the future after their SF Miracle has happened.

REFERENCES

Bannick, R. (2014). *Post-traumatic success*. New York: W.W. Norton, p. 7.

Berg, I. K., & Miller, S. D. (1997). *The miracle method: A radically new approach to problem drinking*. New York: Norton.

Connie, E. (2013). *The Solution-focused marriage: Five simple habits that will bring out the best in your relationship*. The Connie Institute (theconnieinstitute.com).

Dolan, Y. (2000). *Beyond survival: Living well is the best revenge*. London: BT Press.

Dolan, Y. (1991). *Resolving sexual abuse: Solution-focused therapy and Ericksonian hypnosis for survivors*. NY: Norton, p. 40.

Dolan, Y. (1997). I'll start my diet tomorrow: A solution-focused guide to weight loss. *Contemporary Family Therapy*, *19*(1997), 41–48. https://doi.org/10.1023/A:1026106332137.

Dolan, Y. (1998). *One small step: Moving beyond trauma and therapy to a life of joy*. Watsonville, CA: Papier-Mache Press, pp. 77–80.

Duncan, B. (2005). *What's right with you: Debunking dysfunction and changing your life*. Health Communications.

Ghul, R. (2015). *The power of the next small step*. The Connie Institute (theconnieinstitute.com).

Gibson, A. (2020). *Make life simple: Make your life as simple as possible but not simpler*. Wharfedale: Fisher King.

Henden, J. (2011). *Beating combat stress: 101 techniques for recovery*. Wiley.

Henden, J. (2017). *What it takes to thrive: Techniques for severe trauma and stress recovery*. WSPC.

Hudson, P. (1996). *The solution-oriented woman*. New York: Norton.

Metcalf, L. (2004). *The Miracle Question: Answer it and change your life*. Carmarthen Wales: Crown House.

O'Hanlon, B. (2004). *Thriving Through Crisis: Turn Tragedy and Trauma into Growth and Change*. Baltimore, Maryland: Perigree Books.

O'Hanlon, B., & Hudson, P. (1995). *Love is a verb: How to stop analyzing your relationship and start making it great again*. New York: Norton.

Pichot, T., & Dolan, Y. (2003). *Solution-Focused Brief Therapy: It's effective use in agency settings*. NY: Haworth Clinical Practice Press.

Scott, B., Rebolj, B., & Oberbeck, G. (2021) *Beyond coping: Finding your way forward*. London: BT Press.

von Cziffra-Bergs, J. (2018). SFBT and violent crime. In A. S. Froerer, J. von Cziffra-Bergs, J. Kim, & E. Connie (Eds), *Solution-focused brief therapy with clients managing trauma*. New York: Oxford Press, pp. 57–58.

Weiner-Davis, M. (1992) *Divorce busting*. New York: Simon & Schuster.

Weiner-Davis, M. (1996). *Change your life and everyone in it*. New York: Simon & Schuster.

GLOSSARY

Brief psychotherapy   A form of counseling and psychotherapy designed to require less time than more traditional approaches.

Deductive   Theoretically based, typically developed in an academic setting.

Evidence-based   Proven to be effective by credible, substantive scholarly research.

Exceptions   A key element of the SFT approach, exceptions are examples of times when behaviors associated with a specified goal have previously happened.

Goal-Driven   A process in which a goal or pre-defined desired outcome uniquely and ultimately determine which methods or techniques are employed.

Inductive   Developed as a result of direct observation.

Instead questions   Inquiries designed to generate a proactive goal description by identifying people to focus on what they want rather than what they don't want.

The Medical Model   The approach to treating medical problems by using scientific methods to precisely identify the causes of diseases and subsequently identify or develop specific ways to eliminate them.

Paradigmatic Shift   An important change that happens when the usual way of thinking about or doing something is replaced by a new and different way.

Post-traumatic stress   A constellation of symptoms variously characterised by anxiety, depression, sleep disturbance, nightmares, flashbacks, and physiological complaints, occurring in the aftermath of traumatic experiences.

Post Traumatic Stress Disorder (PTSD) A constellation of symptoms occurring in the aftermath of traumatic events variously includes disturbing mental imagery or "flashbacks," and/or nightmares related to traumatic experiences, concentration difficulties, sadness, anger, fearfulness, difficulty relaxing, and/or feeling safe.

SF Assumptions The set of overarching ideas providing the basis for the Solution-Focused approach originally developed by Steve de Shazer, Insoo Kim Berg, and their team of colleagues at the Milwaukee Brief Family Therapy Center.

SF Guidelines The set of practical principles that SF practitioners consistently employ to guide their implementation of the SF approach.

Solution-Focused Compliments Positive statement based on direct observation; these can be directly stated or communicated indirectly.

Solution-Focused Coping Question Question focusing on clients' current, past, and desired level of coping with a specific situation or condition, e.g. *What has helped you to cope with ...* "Or" *How have you managed to cope with or get through other difficult situations in the past?*

Solution-Focused Detail Question An inquiry designed to further clarify various specific aspects of a goal, exception, position on a scale, coping, or solution description.

Solution-Focused Direct Compliment Directly stated positive statement based on direct observation; these can be directly stated or communicated indirectly, e.g. *I am very impressed with how you did that.*

Solution-Focused Exception Question Question designed to elicit detailed descriptions of times when specific behaviors associated with a desired goal have previously happened.

Solution-Focused Goal Development Question An inquiry designed to elicit clients' best hope or desired therapeutic outcome, e.g. *What is your best hope in coming here today, What would need to happen as a result of coming here in order for you to be able to honestly say afterwards that it had been helpful to come,* and other variations. SF Goal Development Questions can take many different forms including *What would tell your best friend (or other person) afterwards that it had been helpful for you to come here today?*

Solution-Focused Indirect Complement Statement in which positive attribution is implied rather than directly stated. Oftentimes this form of compliment is delivered in the form of a question voiced in an appreciative tone, e.g. *How did you do that?*

Solution-Focused Instead Questions Inquiries designed to generate a proactive goal description by identify people to focus on what they want rather than what they don't want.

Solution-Focused Miracle or Best Hope Question A solution-development technique designed to elicit a detailed description of the specific behaviors needed to replace a problem with a solution.

Solution-Focused Miracle Letter from the Future A self-help technique involving writing a detailed future-dated letter describing what one's life is like after the SF Miracle has happened. (This letter is not intended to be mailed, but simply used as a vehicle for exploring the details of a person's preferred future). Following writing the SF Miracle Letter From the Future, an SF scale is employed to identify the steps needed to progress in the direction of the desired future described.

Solution-Focused Miracle or "Problem is Gone" Question A solution-development technique designed to elicit a detailed description of the specific behaviors needed to replace a problem with a solution.

Solution-Focused Safety Net or is there Anything I Forgot to Ask Question A question typically asked before the conclusion of an SF session to ensure that the client has the opportunity to disclose additional information if needed, particularly in reference to any potential issues regarding personal safety.

Solution-Focused Scale A linear diagram showing a 0–10 continuum in which 10 represents the desired goal and 0 represents the opposite or complete absence of the characteristics associated with that goal.

Solution-Focused Scaling Question An evaluative question designed to measure the distance between clients' desired goal and their current state. Scaling questions are based on a literal or imagined linear diagram showing a 0–10 continuum in which 10 represents the desired goal and 0 represents the opposite or complete absence of the characteristics associated with that goal, e.g. *on a scale of 0–10 in which 10 represents that you are completely happy with your current work performance, and 0 represents the opposite, where are you now?*

Solution-Focused Self-Scaling A self-help technique in which people ask themselves Solution-Focused scaling questions in reference to a personal goal.

Solution-Focused Therapy (SFT), also known as Solution-Focused Brief Therapy (SFBT), is a short-term goal-directed evidence-based therapy approach that helps clients change by creating solutions rather than dwelling on problems and the events that led to them.

Solution-Focused What's Better Question A question oftentimes asked by SF practitioners at the beginning of second or subsequent SF sessions.

Solution-Focused What Else Question This is another version of the SF Detail Question specifically designed to elicit descriptions of additional exceptions or further details of a specific SF Exception.

Technique-Driven A process in which technique strongly influences or pre-determines goal selection.

Traditional Psychotherapy Psychotherapy approaches directly directly based on primarily derived from the work of Sigmund Freud.

Trauma Informed A practice that takes into consideration how trauma survivors may respond to words and actions, and provides a safe, supportive environment that fosters empowerment and healing.

INDEX

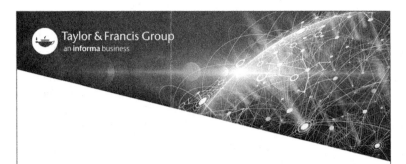

Printed in the United States
by Baker & Taylor Publisher Services